SISTER PARISH DESIGN

St. Martin's Press ❧ *New York*

SISTER PARISH DESIGN

ON DECORATING

SUSAN BARTLETT CRATER &
LIBBY CAMERON

Watercolors by Mita Corsini Bland

www.stmartins.com

Frontispiece: Drawing room designed by Bunny Williams
Murals and illustrations on pages 51 and 154 are by Chuck Fisher
All fabrics and wallpaper designs are by Sister Parish Design

ISBN 978-0-312-38458-6

First Edition: November 2009

10   9   8   7   6   5   4   3   2   1

For my family, Doug, Eliza, and Tuck, with love

—SUSAN BARTLETT CRATER

For Cully, Flora, Charlotte, and Clara, with all my love

—LIBBY CAMERON

CONTENTS

FOREWORD

I am indeed very proud of my friends Susan Crater and Libby Cameron, who have created this amazing book—*Sister Parish Design: On Decorating*. The book explores the various and thought-provoking byways that define the main aspects of decoration today.

Susan, as a granddaughter of the indomitable Sister Parish, shares her personal observations and influences. Libby Cameron, whose professional career was well-grounded by her association with Mrs. Henry Parish II, my late, great friend and partner in Parish-Hadley Associates, draws extensively on that association and her years of experience.

From their shared foundations Susan Crater and Libby Cameron have cast their net far and wide to bring into clear focus the creative ideas and philosophies of some of the foremost decorators in both America and England. The result is brilliant, entertaining, and of paramount authority, accurately reflecting the climate of interior design and decoration in the current century.

ALBERT HADLEY, FEBRUARY 2009

A DRAWING ALBERT HADLEY MADE FOR
LIBBY CAMERON ON HER BIRTHDAY

INTRODUCTION

Many people may consider a book about decorating a frivolous one given our turbulent times, but it seems to me the opposite holds true. I come from a family background with a focus on "design" and the pursuit of creative endeavors. This creativity has never manifested itself in an overemphasis on material possessions, but rather on domesticity and the urge to remove oneself from the day-to-day grind by engaging in activities such as painting, cooking, gardening, and writing—so many of the wonderful things that let you escape into your "home." Creating an imaginative and welcoming refuge for your family and friends, as well as a wonderful diversion from the sometimes tough realities of our world, is a worthwhile pursuit that can only enrich the soul. If one has the financial resources to hire a great decorator, like those who have participated in our book, it will undoubtedly be a creative journey that will be at once an educational and aesthetic delight because of the tremendous creativity that the top decorators bring to a project. If one is doing it alone, decorating can also be a wonderful journey, filled with trial and error but also with satisfaction and aesthetic rewards. The most important legacy of my grandmother Sister Parish is not solely in the realm of wonderful "taste," but rather in the love of domesticity and the desire to create places within which families will laugh, escape, and ultimately love.

—SUSAN BARTLETT CRATER

It's hard for me to believe that I have been decorating for twenty-six years. A day doesn't go by that I don't reflect on how blessed I am to be working at something that I love to do. I am lucky to have had the exposure that I have had—to have been able to see so many incredible, beautiful houses and collections that people have, and to have had all those years at Parish-Hadley, working closely with both Mrs. Parish and Albert Hadley. It was a magical time for me and an incredible experience, and I am eternally grateful for my time there. Even all these years later, I still get that sense of thrill at the beginning of a job when walking into a space, envisioning the possibilities, and then seeing the transformation. My instincts guide me at this point. The years have ingrained that sixth sense of what can work and what won't work; an attention to balance and scale––it's second nature to me now. My youngest daughter, Clara, has the ability to trust her instincts in the same way; just recently when I questioned her choices during a renovation to her bathroom, she answered, "I just know—it feels right." Fixing up a house or an apartment should be a wonderful experience. It should be fun and exciting—there are so many choices and directions to take. But trusting one's instincts is easier for some than for others. If you don't know what you want, it can be immensely frustrating.

The ability to transform a dismal, cheerless, or empty space and create a home has given me an invaluable and worthwhile purpose in life. Nothing is better than getting a phone call or a note of thanks from a client whose family loves their surroundings and expresses how happy their home makes them feel. What is better than knowing that you have been able to provide a cheerful and comfortable place for someone or for a family? After all, it is our private worlds that instill us with a sense of comfort, of happiness and peace, and give us pleasure.

—LIBBY CAMERON

I have been interested in interiors ever since I was little. We lived in a very large villa outside of Florence and the rooms were arranged rather formally. It was built as a hunting lodge for the Medici family and the Corsinis bought it in the sixteenth century. As children we were always ordered outside to play, but on rainy days there were lots of rooms that were never utilized and we used our imaginations by exploring them and playing.

I started drawing my ideal house when I was still quite young. The house was a peasant house of modest proportions with a large pergola, a table and chairs, and a flask of wine. Years later when my daughter was born, I started painting again and a friend asked me to paint a portrait of a living room in Litchfield, Connecticut. I have been painting interiors ever since. I suppose there are those who paint portraits, and then those, like me, who love to see and illustrate what someone has done with a room. Hopefully, this too is a portrait of sorts because, if successful, a room's decor should reflect the personality and style of the occupant. The rooms that I have painted for this book reflect a variety of styles and designs, but to me they all appear to be happy and imaginative rooms, which were a pleasure for me to capture with my paintbrush.

—MITA CORSINI BLAND

LIFESTYLE, PERSONALITY, TASTE,
HIDDEN DESIRES—YOU HAVE TO ANALYZE ALL
THESE THINGS BEFORE YOU CAN START
DESIGNING IN THE CORRECT WAY.
WE BEGIN AT THE BEGINNING.

—SISTER PARISH

OUR ROOMS

When I was in college in New York I had the luxury and good fortune of visiting many spectacular houses with my grandmother Sister Parish when she called on her friends on the weekend. Sunday lunch was a popular time to entertain with her generation, and it is a shame this tradition has gone out of style in our busy lives. Dedicating a block of time to a Sunday lunch means you are really dedicating the entire day to leisure, as a big component of the Sunday lunch is a cocktail before lunch and wine during the meal, rendering you hopeless for whatever afternoon activities you had previously scheduled.

Many of the houses I visited with Sister were unforgettable. Brooke Astor's house in Briarcliff, New York, stands out as the scene of colorful verbal skirmishes between Mrs. Astor and Sister, both very competitive women. It was also the most representative of a way of life we don't see anymore. All of the big houses in the country had pea stone driveways so the sound of cars on gravel was the first impression, followed by the smell of lovely pots of flowers surrounding the front door or wood smoke from the fire within, depending on the season. The door at Mrs. Astor's beautiful Georgian house would be opened by the familiar major domo of the house, whom my grandmother knew well as she visited often. Sister would always call out "hoo hoo," and the response from far away would be "we are in here," meaning in the beautiful large living room or a smaller cozy library that was almost a sun room. Usually a fire would be crackling and drinks offered up—sherry or something light. I remember the feeling of being frozen in time as we sipped our drinks and looked out at the beautiful gardens, chatted about the news of the day, and then went into the dining room for a traditional meal with lots of spirited conversation. Finally, completely satiated, there would be coffee back in the library or living room. Obviously the house's settings were amazing as Sister and Mrs. Astor had collaborated on its beautiful rooms, but more important, in that grand

A CORNER OF SISTER PARISH'S LIVING ROOM AT 920 FIFTH AVENUE HAS A VARIETY AND MIX OF TEXTURES AND FURNITURE.

Georgian house one was made to feel comfortable and welcome. If we sat in the large living room, there were master paintings scattered about, but you never felt intimidated or overwhelmed. Seating arrangements were cozy and the upholstered furniture wonderfully comfortable.

We had similar lunches at the Whitneys' house on Long Island, a rambling Dutch Colonial revival, which embodied a grand, yet livable country house, or her childhood friends' houses in New Jersey, typically smaller clapboard farmhouses filled with odd family heirlooms and bursting with color and charm. No matter the era of the house, the recipe was the same: extremely comfortable living rooms or libraries with brightly colored chintz and a mix of assorted eclectic family paintings and objects, delicious three-course meals that began with piping hot soups and finished with old-fashioned cakes and custards, and throughout, attention to the moment—no rushing to finish and get going. I don't think I ever saw anyone from that generation rush. It must have been considered very bad manners.

The rooms that we visited in these great houses were well worn and well lived in. You had the impression that countless parties, family meals, or just plain hours of reading the Sunday paper had taken place in these rooms. That is what good decorating is—the transformation of a house to be aesthetically beautiful as well as useful for the family that lives there. Comfort and lack of intimidation were the foundation these houses were built on. It was not unusual to see a typically tattered dog bed underneath an old master painting. The rooms were designed to be used and they were, to their fullest.

Billy Baldwin was a great proponent of urging his clients to live in their living rooms and he paid homage to Sister's living room in his discussion, "How to live in a living room," from the book *Billy Baldwin Decorates,* which includes some effective pointers:

> *When it comes to color think warm. Deep vibrant colors like brown, red, or burnt orange make a room intimate without reducing its size. I like to see furniture covered with chintz in a traditional room or with a wonderful contemporary pattern in a more modern room. I love to see*

objects around—not a clutter, but enough so everyone knows these rooms belong to someone—things happen here. One of the nicest living rooms in New York belonged to one of my colleagues, Mrs. Henry Parish II, who knows just how to live in a living room. The walls were dark brown. The curtains were the color of coral and there was wonderful English garden chintz on all of the big overstuffed chairs and sofas. She had arranged the furniture in three groups—one of them around the fire. Here was where she sat every day to have a cup of tea and read the mail. Here was where the family gathered drawn by the firelight on chilly afternoons. The room was equally beautiful when filled with people or when you were alone there. That is what I call a room that's lived in.

—SUSAN BARTLETT CRATER

LIVING ROOMS

Madame used to say, "We are not decorating—we are making places to live."

WILLIAM HODGINS

LIBBY CAMERON When we started with projects at Parish-Hadley, there was never a moment given to the possibility that any one of the rooms would not be used and loved and lived in. Each room was as important as the next although the purpose may have been different. And as I learned well, each room has to connect to the others, not in terms of the colors used, but in its aesthetic; each room needs to be its own while simultaneously being part of a whole. I remember Mrs. Parish talking about rooms and colors swearing at each other, and the importance of a thread that tied all of the rooms together. Comfort is an element that connects rooms and is what Parish-Hadley was known for. A room was never designed without thought given to how it would be used and what was important, how the light fell and how many people lived there, how the lamps or lighting in the room would draw you in and enable you to read. Living rooms were never planned with just one place to sit and often had three or more seating areas, and were cozy enough so that one or many people could be comfortable. Parish-Hadley was a wonderful school for so many. Ingrained in us all was the importance of imaginative warm rooms that had to be friendly, comfortable, and timeless.

MITCHELL OWENS What I think the "graduates" of Parish-Hadley have in common is a certain respect for history without being slavish, a breadth of vision that reveres quality over specific periods or styles, and an understanding of real comfort, no matter how formal the client's lifestyle. I don't think I've ever been in a room executed by a Parish-Hadley alum that isn't eminently livable. The rooms themselves may not be my cup of tea, per se, in terms of

MILES REDD USES COLOR AND TEXTILES TO CREATE A WARM AND INVITING LIVING ROOM.

looks, but the comfort level is pretty much steady across the board, don't you think? There's inherent practicality, too, an attention to the sorts of amenities that many designers of otherwise striking rooms often forget. (There is a world of difference between a room styled to be beautiful and a room that is actually decorated for living.) I once spent an evening at a star designer's apartment, and though the sitting room was spectacularly outfitted, I had to clutch my glass all evening—there was no place to set a drink down! That sort of foolishness would never occur in a room with a Parish-Hadley bloodline. At least, I hope not.

MARIO BUATTA The thing about English houses that is so great is that they are always played down with chintz and sisal carpeting. Sister did the same thing. She did not like a room that was only filled with "important furniture."

JANE CHURCHILL Obviously I come from a family of decorators, being Nancy Lancaster's niece; Nancy's sister, my grandmother Alice Winn, never worked as a decorator, but she had fantastically good taste and always did it much more on a shoestring. She could turn a hovel into something. I remember the house she had at Sandwich—a really nasty, suburban-looking brick house. By the time she added lattice balconies to it, painted it a different color, and planted a garden in front of it, it was drop-dead gorgeous. But she always did it in a much cheaper way than Aunt Nancy, not that money with Aunt Nancy was key. I will always remember she had something red in every room. They both had an eye for things that some people didn't seem to see. I think you are born with an eye or you're not. Nancy Lancaster and Alice Winn had incredibly wonderful, comfortable houses with bathrooms that always looked like other people's drawing rooms and my grandmother always had very, very good food. They were American. We were brought up with American backgrounds, not just a British background. In those days comfort was more unique. My cousin Lady Wissie Ancaster had wonderful taste, but that also came because she had the whole line of Aunt Nancy, Granny, and the whole lot in her. They didn't just make homes, they made wonderful homes. They were never pretentious.

Nothing was ever pretentious. Dogs were everywhere, pee stains on the edge of the curtains. Not that it was ever dirty, but they were absolutely lacking in any form of pretention. They were such personalities themselves. The women had such energy.

Nancy Lancaster was funny and amusing and she treated everyone the same, from a duke to the dustman, and they all adored her. She was really happy in her garden with all the gardeners. The staff she had was there for years and they all adored her because she was kind and funny. She always had an eclectic group of people around her. They were just very talented.

EMMA BURNS When I was working with Roger Banks-Pye, we were on the way to see a client and he said we should make a quick detour and go see Nancy. We had a delicious lunch—this was when she was at the Coach House at Haseley—and that was just enchanting. She must have been about eighty-seven by then—she said a hundred minus thirteen. She was quite wonderfully eccentric.

Sadly, I only met her that one time and I never met John Fowler. He was very much the decorator and she sort of dabbled really. She had most of the contacts. Also she had that phenomenal American style. It was the combination of her and John Fowler together that was so exciting. She had the confidence and he had the attention to detail. You think of a room like the Yellow Room at Brook Street and people always make the mistake of saying that that strength of color was an American influence, but it's pure John Soane. I think that she was brilliant at using color when most people had rather forgotten about colors or using them on a grander scale. There was also always something informal about her interiors. They were lived-in. They didn't have the stilted feeling that so much English decoration had. They are not formulaic, but with individual pieces and collections of things, not studied in any way.

PETER DUNHAM I am concerned about creating spaces that people are actually going to inhabit, places where they are going to want to go into that corner and read, for example. I am focused on what's going to bring them into the room. How am I going to make this living room work? So I am very concerned about creating destination places in my decorating. The big challenge here in LA is that there are all these nightmare windows and doors. There is no way to do the destination thing with that kind of architecture so I am always moving doors slightly and closing things out so that there are actual places that people will want to go. That's where I start—figuring out the use. With the client we also spend weeks talking about whether they like to watch TV in bed or whether they like toilet paper on the left-hand side or the right-hand side. Finally, they get a feeling that you understand their physical needs.

JEFFREY BILHUBER I always think comfort will override surprise or astonishment. Perhaps the most astonishing thing is when a house continues to reward and give back to you as you use it. That is going to have a more long-lasting effect than anything else.

PETER DUNHAM I think that people want to go to a glamorous house and they want it to be exciting. On the other hand, they don't want to be intimidated by it. So you've got to take the air out of it. There is nothing worse than going to a house and thinking, "Oh my god, this is very fancy." People are scared to sit on the sofa. It happens all the time. It's too rich. Sister's genius was at making people feel it's okay to be in their houses and have the confidence that the people were more interesting than the houses.

For me it's like dressing people—you've got to make the clients look and feel sexy. So if I have a forty-five-year-old single studio executive from Paramount, I want him to be sexy when he has a date. I want him to impress people if he wants to. Also, if someone is coming from a date, I want him to be able to curl up on the sofa and end up in bed with the person. That's what he wants. You've got to make him look slimmer and taller. You've got to make him look fun and eclectic and amusing, and have a sense of humor. My clients call me up and say the house is so great and people love coming. If it's a drab depressing house it's such a downer—who wants to go there?

The essential thing is the function and how to bring people in to use the room and how to break that room to humanize it. Also how you build in mistakes so it doesn't look like it's absolutely perfect and lifeless. For example, in a very fancy silk velvet living room you might want to have a dog bed or something, just so that it feels like somebody is actually living there. You make sure to include a desk so that's where someone goes to use the computer—and have the bills piled up, rather than it be two sofas and be perfect. Sister and Nancy Lancaster were very strong in making people understand about living in houses.

TODD ROMANO I have a theory that if most people had a huge open kitchen, living room, sitting room, and an office they would be happy. I think many houses and apartments nowadays are underused. I tend to make rooms where people will feel comfortable and use them. We try to make living rooms very inviting, for example. Our parents and our grandparents used those rooms because people entertained much more. Nobody really entertains very much anymore. One of my great friends and also a client, Cornelia, is one of the few young ladies I know who still really entertains—luncheon parties, dinner parties—at home. You think of all the people we know and with such amazing resources available to them in these massive apartments and they won't even have you over for a peanut butter or tuna fish sandwich. It's insane. It's a funny thing because growing up in South Texas—San Antonio—we didn't go to restaurants. Most of my mother's family is from Virginia and Georgia. Part of her family left after the Civil War and settled in Corpus Christi. My mother grew up in San Antonio and there was a lot of holdover from the Georgia-Virginia Southern lifestyle, which was then adapted to the heat of South Texas. Sunday dinners were always a big thing. The concept of entertaining at home was very important to my grandmother and my mother both. My grandmother was, and my mother still is, an exceptional gardener with a huge interest in horticulture and landscape gardening. My father and I come from a long line of Italian engineers and builders. We are all frustrated architects and what Italian doesn't like to stack rocks? I grew up in a house that was always changing. There were always additions being done inside or out, gardens being planned, patios being laid. Our family lived in one house for about twenty-eight or thirty years and that house went through so many transformations. It evolved over time. As our family grew and changed, the house grew and changed to accommodate it.

MILES REDD I believe in big living rooms. Big, cozy living rooms that are full of objects are better with more seating areas. How do we get twenty people sitting in this living room? I always think about how you are going to live and what makes sense for a group or a gathering of people, which is very much a Southern way of thinking. But it's not exclusively Southern. I don't know why we get all the credit. I have met some awful nice Yankees. I want people to feel welcome. You were invited—I like you—make yourself at home and relax. I think that comes more from the personality of the person who invited you. There is perfection in imperfection. You want some things to be a little off. When things are perfect it feels like Disney World in a way.

PAUL VINCENT WISEMAN A house is a reflection of your soul. It is the most personal reflection. Think about it—you can buy the right jewelry, the right neighborhood, the right car, the right clothes, and the right hairdo. Guess what? When someone walks into your house it's scary. It's very scary, particularly to people who don't come from strong cultural backgrounds. Because they know they're going to be judged.

MARTHA ANGUS I do not necessarily try to get as much seating in a room as possible. I like air around things. I like space. The Bronfmans' apartment was one of my favorites. It was beautiful because it had air around objects. I prefer that. I also think that to function you need to have a place to put a drink down and to be able to read a book.

SMALL SPACES

There is a wonderful kind of magic that small spaces can have.

LIBBY CAMERON

LIBBY CAMERON My first office at Parish-Hadley was quite literally a closet that had its door removed, with a built-in desk with a bulletin board above it on one side and bookshelves floor to ceiling on the other. It was maybe six feet long and three feet deep, but it was cozy, a very cozy little nook to work in. All of the decorators at Parish-Hadley decorated their offices. I didn't have much to decorate, but I did choose a wallpaper from the Parish-Hadley archives; it was red and white, an all-over pattern with a ribbon around the line of the ceiling.

TODD ROMANO In my house in Millbrook I have the most wonderful little room. It was this odd room that was in between my library and my entrance hall. It had been used as an office. I had another window cut in the room and I had the walls lined with books. The only other thing I did was put in a daybed. I would lie on that bed and talk on the telephone and read books, take a nap— and I loved it. It was a little hideaway and it was great. I am a big reader, as you can tell, and right now my cozy little space is probably my bed at home. I read in bed a lot at night. My walls in my bedroom are lined with the same sort of felt but in dark brown and that is a cozy little area I love.

SUSAN BARTLETT CRATER Sister loved little rooms as much as big rooms. In Maine she had old houses, which are, of course, usually dominated by smallish rooms. In the Red House she painted all of the small rooms dark colors, like eggplant or deep blue, to make them appear bigger. She was very much for dark, richly painted high-gloss walls in smaller rooms. They would have a bold contrasting white trim and usually a great rag rug, but she was never apologetic about her treatment of the smallest of rooms. She put big

gutsy furniture in them and they were very livable. My favorite small room was the guest room at 960 Fifth Avenue, where I used to stay. It was tucked in off the living room in a space so small it was practically a closet. Despite its size, it had so many minute magical elements and such a comforting array of feminine colors, you felt like a princess when staying there. She always had the most amazing ancient linen sheets that were laundered to "perfection," as she would say—the bed practically swallowed you up it was so comfortable. The combination of the delicate colors (the palest pink walls, celery green chintz, light beige rug), and the utter comfort of its details magically conspired to create a delicious haven for anyone lucky enough to stay there.

LIBBY CAMERON Mrs. Parish had a little guest room in her apartment at 960 Fifth. It was so tiny that only a twin bed and a night table fit in the space. It was filled with charm. We were to leave on a trip very early one morning to visit a client, and Mrs. Parish insisted that I spend the night. When she insisted on something, it was almost impossible not to do as she asked. I loved my night in that little room, it was such a cozy happy little room. It had one window that was originally a door, curtains of chintz with carnations and beaded fringe, an upholstered headboard, and a dust drop of a different chintz pattern and a multicolored quilt on the bed. The night table was painted. The carpeting had a small geometric pattern, and there was a little hooked rug on top of it. The walls were painted and there was a floral wallpaper border around the top of the room. When in bed, you could touch the wall across from the bed. It was the most wonderful little room.

BUNNY WILLIAMS Storage is the biggest problem of all in small spaces. You may start out with nothing, but eventually you are going to have stuff. If you have a small room, you probably want one big sofa and one other thing to balance that sofa, and then you fill in with smaller things. For example, if I

A BAR SET UP ON AN ANTIQUE DESK IS A CASUAL AND INVITING PLACE FOR GUESTS TO HELP THEMSELVES TO A DRINK.

had a small library, I would have a good-size sofa and probably across from it something like a bookcase or a cabinet to balance it. Then I would put smaller things with it. If you have to have a seven-foot sofa and a huge chair that the husband wants—or two of those—all of a sudden it is going to make this room seem smaller and cramped. You really have to go out and find comfortable chairs that aren't so huge. I think many people just go sit in a chair in a store like Pottery Barn and they say, "Oh, this chair is so comfortable," and they buy it. When they get it home they realize it's too big. They are seeing it in a vast space and not imagining how this chair that's 40 inches deep by 36 inches wide is going to work in their tiny room.

SUSAN BARTLETT CRATER In our family we are fans of multipurpose small rooms or changing the makeup of a small room to get full use out of it. My Uncle Harry's room in Maine was known as "the black hole of Calcutta" when my mother was young because of its dark interior and messy treatment. As soon as he was out of the house, it became a laundry and he was put upstairs. The guest room next to it became a card-room-slash-library and then back to a guest room when we finally admitted no one played cards or did puzzles, for that matter, as much as my grandmother dreamed they would. She was also a big proponent of taking her afternoon nap in a room other than her bedroom. There are two big Aiken sofas in Maine—one in the dining room and the other in a guest room. She always had the best cashmere blankets on them and she would alternate between the two for her daily nap in the summer. It was always the running joke that the minute she fell asleep someone would start mowing the lawn outside her window.

The size of a house or rooms was never a big concern for her. It was of more concern whether there was light, and ultimately, how practical the house or apartment would be. Dark rooms with no light or impractical houses that could never work for a family's or a single person's needs were characterized as "fatal," her worst insult.

THE UNDERUSED
DINING ROOM

You really have to know a lot about people and how they live. Where do they have dinner? If they don't entertain, why use the dining room for dinner parties for fourteen people who are never going to show up? Do something else interesting with it. BUNNY WILLIAMS

LIBBY CAMERON Dining rooms so often feel like forgotten rooms to me. They are used less often today as people entertain less and space is so valuable. People don't always eat at a table anymore, and instead have dinner on a tray in another room altogether. Colors, wallpaper, and the decorative strength of pattern can make a dining room cozier, but having more than just a sideboard, table, and chairs will make it a more practical room. Having books and comfortable places to sit will change the room altogether, yet it still works as a dining room when it needs to be just that. But in the meantime, it can also serve as just another cozy place to be.

BUNNY WILLIAMS There is this convention: oh, I have a dining room, so I have to put the table in it. I say, don't do that. Okay, if you are going to use it as a dining room, fine. But you could make it the library and do something else with the library, if there is one. Just use your house in a way that is useful to you.

JANE CHURCHILL I have a dining room that is also a library. It's quite big—somebody calls it my ballroom—but is my library, dining room, and hall. Dining rooms can be ridiculous today. Who is going to use them unless you have a staff?

EMMA BURNS DESIGNED A DELIGHTFUL AND INVITING DINING ROOM IN LONDON
USING AN ECLECTIC MIX OF FURNITURE, RICH COLORS, CHARMING OBJECTS,
AND PAINTINGS. THE VARIETY OF CHAIRS ADDS TO THE INTEREST OF THE ROOM.

ALBERT HADLEY I like to encourage people to combine the dining room and make it a room that is used. Perhaps it contains a collection of things—or maybe the best solution is to make it into a library. You can add bookcases and still have your dining table, but there are more ways to use the room. You can have the dining table at one end of the room, and if it's a living room combination, then you can make the other end more of an area where you gather around.

EMMA BURNS Dining rooms are rooms that sometimes need to double up as another room; libraries and dining rooms are obviously wonderful together. I love playing with table settings and I love family china and glass. I love mixing old and new and antique pieces. At home I have endless dinner services and I have antique plates that I use for different courses. I enjoy mixing old and new and it also makes the food look so good. So dining rooms are hugely important.

An issue I have with newly built houses is that people don't have enough space to eat properly. I am not talking about good big houses. I am talking about affordable housing—the dining room doesn't exist and the kitchens are often not quite big enough for people to eat in. It all contributes to the breakdown of family life—look at the French who close their businesses from noon to 2 p.m. in order to eat lunch. I think it's a huge shame when homes don't have a place big enough to eat in comfortably with your family and your friends because it's such a fantastic part of life. One might have a sofa or banquette on one side of the table, perhaps flanked with bookcases, so the room doesn't look like a dining room waiting to happen. But it does have the feeling of a library and it would be able to turn easily into a dining room at meal times.

I also love the idea of not having a complete set of dining chairs. Nancy Lancaster did this. She would often have a pair of tall and skinny wing chairs at the head of the table and single chairs around it. That is what she had at the Coach House at Haseley and it was enchanting—so lovely and comfortable. It made a very small dining room feel much more grand.

Dining rooms can often feel like dead rooms. Quite often people don't have a nice dining table so I will just make the table out of chipboard and put a floor-length cloth over it and overlay this with another cloth on top for dining. That can look fantastic and the focus will become the chairs around the table. You can paint chairs and cover them in endless different ways. I did a job where we had the prettiest dining room of all time. It had a table with a skirt on it, and then another cloth over that, and the dining chairs were little French park chairs with very simple beige and white ticking—it was divine. This was in the grandest apartment in Knightsbridge, very good address, etc., but it had this real quirky charm. It was very, very pretty.

CARLETON VARNEY For Dorothy Draper, the dining room was theater and she entertained as if it were theater. She had an apartment in the Carlyle, one of those big ones with the very tall ceilings. Dorothy had a social secretary at the apartment, who handled her social life. She would keep a list of everyone who ever came for dinner, how D.D. set the table, who sat next to whom, and so on, so no one sat next to the same person the next time. She also kept card files on everybody and how they behaved as dinner guests, menus as well—everything was catalogued.

In the dining room, the walls were a plum purple, deeper than aubergine. She had a great big console table, with a beautiful gold base and a solid green malachite top. All the chairs were in a very bright black and gold and with tufted raspberry satin upholstery. There was also a fabulous mirror—a great big Venetian mirror. The window treatment fabric was a creamy color with another under curtain, which I remember because I still use that fabric today. It was wide-striped raw silk. The curtains were always drawn at night. There were two great big urns filled with flowers. There were, of course, a lot of candles and always music.

BEDROOMS

My philosophy with bedrooms is, if you are only going to do one room in your house, do the bedroom first. I have told this to many clients. It's where you spend the greatest amount of time—it's what you see first thing in the morning and the last thing at night. The whole house can be disruptive, but to have your bedroom finished is going to add a calming sense to your life.

SUZANNE TUCKER

LIBBY CAMERON I worked on a bedroom years ago that was glazed in a raspberry red crosshatch pattern in squares. The walls were very textural and the bed and the curtains were made out of chintz from Fortuny, which no longer exists. It had a red and white stripe that looked like twisted and knotted fabric, on a very white ground. The combination of the walls and the crispness of the fabric was very pretty. The room didn't have fussiness to it—it was tailored and strong. Bedrooms can be tricky in that they should be rooms to not only sleep in but to sit in and really live in. I love having a seating area in a bedroom—it makes it warm and cozy.

MARIO BUATTA Men love to be romantic. Men are also afraid of what other men are going to say about them. Most of the time they haven't got a clue. When I give a lecture I always ask the men in the audience what color their bedrooms are and they never know. I had a client once who said her husband wouldn't sleep in a room filled with flowered chintz. She had six windows in her bedroom and we did two at a time. Do you know when he realized he had new curtains? Not until the bill came. He never noticed the curtains. They don't notice anything. I did a bedroom at Kips Bay, a blue bedroom with a sheer white canopy bed, and a client wanted me to get her the same bed. She had recently met a man from Sweden and they had gotten married and bought a new house. She told me that she had always wanted a bed like the one in the show house. I said okay and we did it. The new husband walks in—he was a very macho Swedish man with his briefcase—and he sees this canopy bed with all of the stuff and he asks, "Do men sleep in beds like this?" I was shaking I was so nervous. The tassels on my loafers were trembling and I said, "Uh-oh." I called them all weekend—I could never get them. The housekeeper, who was new, kept saying, "I am sorry, Mr. Buatta, I can't disturb them." I said, "What's going on," and she said, "Well, they are resting. They are in the bedroom suite." So I called again the next day and they were still not taking any calls. I said, "Are they eating?" She said, "I bring up the tray and they seem to be nourished." So I called the office Monday morning and was told she'd be in at twelve, and at twelve on the button she called and said, "What are you doing, trying to kill me?" I asked what had happened. "Did the canopy fall down?" She said, "He fell on the bed on Friday night and never got out—it was the most romantic thing that ever happened to me!"

SUZANNE TUCKER If you are married, believe me it will make husbands much happier, because when all else fails, if the bedroom is calm and pretty and beautifully done, it makes a big difference. Clients have said: "You told me to do my bedroom first, and I thought you were crazy because I just wanted to get my living room done, but you were so right." It's one of those revelations. If you are only going to do one room, do your bedroom first. We all love our bedrooms.

Oftentimes it's true, women want a more feminine color. I usually try to coax a husband to coming around to that thinking. Bedrooms should be more feminine and I always tell a husband a man should feel like he is coming into a woman's bedroom. There is something very sexy and seductive and intimate about that. Most men like that idea and I have had the most macho men in pink bedrooms. A lot of men don't like canopy beds because they feel claustrophobic in them. They are beautiful but a lot of men do react against them. It's on a primal level. They don't want to be enclosed. If I can't talk someone into

A BEDROOM DESIGNED BY MARIO BUATTA CENTERS AROUND A MAGNIFICENT
CANOPY BED, WHICH CREATES A SENSE OF ROMANCE AND LUXURY.

a canopy, I talk them into a half canopy. A lot of the time they don't want something over their head.

MARIO BUATTA I have been sleeping on a canopy bed since my third apartment, which was on 62nd Street. You feel like you're in your little world. Those Hollywood beds that are king-size are hideous. It's a whole sea of mattress.

ALBERT HADLEY One of the reasons we started to help Betsey Whitney at Greentree was because Princess Margaret and Lord Snowden were coming to visit. Betsey Whitney called us because the wing of the house they were going to put them in was a wreck. The rooms were storerooms really. We got in there and pulled it all together and made the rooms work. There was a big discussion between Betsey, Sis, and myself about their bedroom. Sis was saying there was a beautiful pair of twin beds and the girls were going to put them in those. I said you can't do that—do you know what you are doing? They have just gotten married! I finally won.

EMMA BURNS I always picture how someone is going to look in their bed. It's terribly important. I have to make sure that it is deeply flattering. I think bedrooms should be restful. I don't think that that necessarily means that they can't have wonderful colors in them. It's about the way you use the fabrics, wall colors, the shape of the room, and the balance of the objects in it. I quite like a lot of symmetry in a bedroom, which is always very calming. When you're lying in your bed, it's very lovely to look at a pair of windows with a painting or a mirror between them, over a piece of furniture. That's a very lovely, very calm elevation. Order is good. I believe in order, anyway. You have to have fantastic storage because that allows you to be ordered—otherwise your life is too difficult. You have to make it easy on yourself.

ALBERT HADLEY'S BEDROOM REPRESENTS HIS SPARE USE OF OBJECTS
AND HIS VIVID USE OF COLOR.

Mita Corsini Bland

Mita Corsini Bland

THE ENTRY

The element of surprise is really important in a front hall.

BRIAN McCARTHY

LIBBY CAMERON The entrance into a house is like the preface to a book; it should give you a sense of what you are entering, but not tell the whole story. It is the link, or cog pin, which holds the house together. Whether it is a small foyer or a proper entrance hall, it has to have character and poise, and set a tone. Depending on the project, Parish-Hadley treated the entrance as its own entity. We always discussed what the floors should be and how to create an inviting yet practical place in which to arrive. There was always a front hall table with a lamp, a place to put down your keys, a mirror to look into as you enter or exit, an overhead lantern, and a place to hang your hat.

BRIAN McCARTHY I have clients out on the Island who have this incredible view of Long Island Sound. Initially the house was designed with this enormous opening—I mean a huge front hall that you walk into that leads into a big drawing room with this huge view. Everybody from the get-go started with the idea that you walk in the house and see the water. I said no, let's walk into the house and not give it all away at first glance. First you've got this wonderful big stone entry hall, and it really should be about the entry experience, to draw you in and then you move on to the next room. It took months, but gradually the opening to the living room kept getting smaller and smaller. It was a natural evolution. Initially the architect was against it and the client was against it. The client really just didn't get it and kept saying, "But we're building this house on the water, we want to see it." I said you're going to see it when you go into the room. You're going to have all of these fabulous experiences if you go from

THIS LARGE-SCALE LATTICE "TREILLAGE DE BAMBOO" WALLPAPER GIVES THIS STAIR HALL A WONDERFUL SENSE OF PROPORTION.

one room to the other, and it shouldn't just be all about the water view. There should be an element of surprise.

LIBBY CAMERON On a rainy, horrible February day, you don't necessarily want to be looking out at stormy gray water with whitecaps.

MARIO BUATTA Albert taught me about keeping halls austere, unfriendly, and not that inviting. The whole point is in the hall you are waiting to be invited into the sitting room or living room. He thinks they should be cold. When you arrive in someone's hall—we are talking about a big hall in a country house—it's impersonal, it's not warm. It's cold as if they don't want you to stay there that long. It is a place where you greet someone for two minutes. I always think of the hall as the core of the house—the place where you can use blue, you can use green for grass, yellow for sunshine, beige—but it shouldn't be too friendly. Like lobbies of buildings in New York, where they decorate the hall to look like a library, which is so dumb. They think it is a room, but it's not.

JANE CHURCHILL I have a hall fetish. That's the one thing you don't get in London houses. I think halls are absolutely key. First of all, they make a house look bigger. I have just done a house—it is tiny, but it has this really nice hall with a wider than expected staircase. It just makes all the difference. It's no different from the first time you see somebody. It's like your appearance—whatever people say, it matters. It jolly well does. Appearance is key. In the front hall now we have a coat cupboard, with a circle mirror next to it. You have to have a table in the hall with lamps on it, and a mirror and also something to put your keys on so you never lose them. I have put rugs down on the floor, but in London houses, I think it's nice to have wood or stone because it doesn't get filthy. I had a stenciled floor in my last hall, which my nanny did. I had an Australian nanny who was very good at painting. As the children were in school all day, I asked if she would take on the job of painting the floor. She did a lot of that for me.

PAUL VINCENT WISEMAN I did a front hall in Hawaii. The house is right on the beach with the most amazing view, but I said no, that's not the first thing you are going to see. You see the Buddha on the stone table. I filtered it. I used this huge screen—you see, it doesn't give away the whole story. Remember when women's dresses started to get short? All of a sudden there was no interest. Look back in the teens: it was the ankle, then the knee. Did you see *Atonement*? The love scene was the best love scene I have seen in years. Nobody took off their clothes. It was the sexiest dress I have ever seen. It was so hot and the actors were fully clothed. The front hall is like that—don't show too much. This is an intellectual exercise. *Here kitty kitty* is the phrase I use all the time with the entry.

EMMA BURNS The front hall sets the tone of the house, doesn't it? I am passionate about flowers. Flowers or plants and a fireplace—that is very welcoming.

BUNNY WILLIAMS The front hall is important because when you open the door of a house, it pulls you in or it doesn't. It's the first thing you see and it's fun to have a little drama about it. That's why I love to do stenciled or painted floors. You often stand in a front hall. It's your first impression and I think it is a place that should be exciting. It is a great place for a wonderful color; it is a great place for a fabulous floor. It doesn't have to have a lot of furniture in it; I just make sure to have a hall table and a mirror and a beautiful container of flowers. This weekend I cut rhubarb and white tulips. It's the place to welcome

THE FRONT HALL IN SUSAN CRATER'S HOUSE IS DOMINATED BY THE SISTER PARISH DESIGN WALLPAPER "KINNICUTT" AND A MUCH-USED DECOUPAGE UMBRELLA STAND.

people, so make it feel special. Even if I didn't have flowers any other place in the house, I would want them in the front hall.

SUZANNE RHEINSTEIN We have a huge entrance hall with a piano in it. If you were to come to dinner tonight, you would see there is always someone playing the piano in it. It's a great way to welcome people when you have a party. The floor is wood and it's covered with a patchwork of Persian rugs that go up the stairs. I have a big, wonderful nineteenth-century British portrait of a family and this terrific clock that we got on one of our first trips to England together. My husband loves it and it chimes. Some pretty mirrors, a pair of portraits. It's also where my husband and I exercise with our trainer three days a week. We don't have machines but we bring out the mats and we do Pilates and other exercises.

Another entrance hall I really liked belongs to two young writers—it was published in *Elle Decor*. It was a long, narrow one so we just emphasized that and painted it spinach green. Its look is about its being a passageway, and it's made more interesting by some African artifacts. Then you come into this big living room that is light, in a different shade of green. If it's a country house then it could almost be a living hall—with comfortable furniture like a big old sprawl sofa where the dog lives. That can be charming and wonderful, too.

Dorothy's entry hall at the Carlyle was very wide with a black-and-white floor and on the walls a large-scale wallpaper with a huge ribbon design in red and great big roses all over it. She was never without fresh flowers—she spent thousands and thousands of dollars on fresh flowers every month. On the right side of the entry hall was the library, which had dark bottle green on white flocked wallpaper with bright tangerine orange curtains.

OTHER ROOMS

I think kitchens should be kitchens.   BUNNY WILLIAMS

SUSAN BARTLETT CRATER Sister was very concerned about food and menus, but she was not interested in gadgets or brand-name appliances in kitchens. She would think the current preoccupation with stove or refrigerator brands was ludicrous. In Maine she had a kitchen formula that she used in every house. The wooden or linoleum floors were painted with some sort of great design, there was a red-and-white-checked oilcloth on every kitchen table and some sort of collection of very good folk art paintings would decorate the walls. The pantry would be stocked with several sets of beautiful plates, bowls, serving dishes, and glasses from New York. We associated the china in each house or in her New York apartment with the character of the house and the meals that were served on them.

She was obsessed that the food that came out of the kitchen was "piping hot." Menus were planned for weeks and, as they were for most people of her generation, restaurants were foreign places where the choices and menus overwhelmed her. She wanted to be current so we suffered through several awkward meals at "in" places, where she would try to order "off" the menu, like "lemon ice and scrambled eggs," much to the waiter's dismay. Clubs and familiar restaurants like Mortimer's were fine, but she never really relaxed in them. For her, food and entertaining belonged at home, not in public places. She was also incredibly concerned that whoever was doing the cooking was happy. The trials and tribulations of her housekeepers were legendary, and they always became members of the family despite some fiery moments. She would go far to make sure they had everything they needed in the kitchen.

EMMA BURNS I love those really beautiful Italian kitchens, but I like the minimalism to be cut by having a funny sort of country table in the center to contrast with the "chic." I hate it when a room is all one extreme. I love marble for the countertops. I love natural materials. Floors in kitchens—they can be wooden or tiles or anything, really. I think anything goes.

PETER DUNHAM I tend to strive for simplicity. My parents' house in Spain didn't have any electricity or running water when I was growing up. They had the theory that the more stuff you had, the more things would go wrong, things that you would have to fix and need to find a plumber for. That was nonexistent in our village. They were believers in the concept that the more you have that is complicated, the more your life is complicated by maintaining it. I like cooking so I think about things in the kitchen my clients may not have thought of, like always have two dishwashers. I'm terribly lazy and I hate emptying the dishwasher so I wait for the cleaning lady to do it.

I just did this job where they wanted the blender to come up via a hydraulic system from underneath the counter. I was like, this is never going to work—just put it on the counter or put it underneath and just lift it. You are forty years old, you can lift it yourself! There is a lot of that going back and forth. In terms of bathrooms—yes, it's nice to have a steam shower or it's nice to have a bathtub. To me there's not that much technology you need. Radiant floors underneath are very nice. We live in California, and the one thing you learn and the one thing my lovely boyfriend taught me is that a sense of comfort (which I didn't necessarily have) is important. I've learned that working in Los Angeles. People like comfort. The clients want comfort. They want soft fabrics and they want chenille and they want the press of a button. They want ease and comfort.

DANIEL ROMUALDEZ I don't cook as much as I would like to now. There are two schools of thought so I ask my clients, who does the cooking? I have clients that never cook because they have a cook and they never go in to their kitchens. In this case I talk to the cook. We also have clients who actually cook and live in the kitchen, and the whole family is there. That kitchen is

A QUINTESSENTIALLY CHARMING AND LUXURIOUS ENGLISH BATHROOM
DESIGNED BY EMMA BURNS HAS INTERESTING ARTWORK AND OBJECTS, MAKING
IT FEEL MORE LIKE A ROOM AND NOT JUST SIMPLY A BATHROOM.

the most fun to do because it's also the sitting room. You really have to tweak it so that someone can be cooking and the kids can be eating, but you need to have some privacy. You have to have some sort of separation. I find it really disconcerting to be a guest in that kind of home where you are eating in the kitchen with the host, but someone is clanking away at the stove. It should be that they are cooking and you are with them, and then you are sitting down and there is no more activity.

I like things either to disappear completely or have them be honest and functional.

BUNNY WILLIAMS Kitchens should not be overdecorated. The best-looking kitchens have white cabinets, a great practical countertop, and lots of storage. You are in it so much and so many things happen in the kitchen that I don't like themed kitchens. I believe the simpler, the better. Your clients are going to be happier with this and they will never get tired of it. I like wood floors and I like bamboo floors, which are fabulous and very practical. I don't like a hard floor like tile or marble, because if you drop a glass, for example, it shatters. It's also hard to stand on, and it's noisy. It can be a painted wood floor or a stained wood floor. I have to say Antique makes the best-looking wood vinyl you have ever seen. I have it in my kitchen here in New York. It's linoleum strips that look like wood. My kitchen is not huge, but it looks like it has a wonderful rich wood floor. Even Gil Schaefer, who is the biggest purist, got down on his hands and knees and said, "I can't believe it's vinyl!"

I personally prefer countertops to be neutral because I don't want to get tired of them. I have done every kind of countertop. For example, right now someone I'm working with wants green, and I am actually putting in an onyx one. There is a stone which I can't get anymore—it's American granite and it looks more like a soapstone. For a light countertop, I like honed Carrara marble. It's what they put in all of the old kitchens. It's beautiful and classic.

You have to make your house function. When people come in, if you don't have a bar, it is nice to have a tray with sodas, wine, glasses, and an ice bucket so that you can be hospitable right away. People are not waiting. What's fun about that is, that then your guests know where it is so they can go help themselves. People need to know right away, when they walk into a room, where to sit. If the furniture is in the right place, they will know that. If it is in the wrong place, they are going to be looking for a chair to pull up. The minute you see someone pulling up chairs you better rearrange your room because you know the furniture isn't in the right place. Nobody should be standing around.

I have gone to people's houses and they are completely disorganized. Dinner is two hours late and they don't know how to serve it. You find yourself practically setting the table and thinking, I wish we hadn't come over. It doesn't have to be like that if you plan ahead a little bit. If you would say: okay, we are going to have pasta and a salad, and we are going to put it on a platter and it is going to be served in the dining room, and everybody will help themselves and then sit down. It is uncomfortable for the guests to be wondering what's going to happen next. If you go in a house and nobody offers you anything to drink or eat—even if it's just a bowl

LIBBY CAMERON KEPT THE ORIGINAL CABINETS IN A KITCHEN IN MAINE. THE PAINTED BLUE FLOOR AND THE ZINC-TOPPED WORKTABLE ADD TO THE CLASSIC LOOK.

of peanuts, it doesn't have to be fancy—you are uncomfortable. John loves pretzels. A bowl of pretzels and a bowl of peanuts are fine. I think that how you make people feel comfortable is your own ability to organize what is going to happen.

JANE CHURCHILL I like kitchens to look a little bit different. In my last house all the cabinets were painted in a big blue check. Here they are stenciled. I don't like these ditzy little cupboards that you can get maybe two and a half plates in. I like floor-to-ceiling cupboards so that you can put all the glasses in one and all the china in the other. So I usually have a carpenter make them. I like them to be functional. The way this one is done here—you could cook for God knows how many people, but it's still cozy just for the two of you. I like bathrooms the way Nancy did them—making them rooms. I can remember one of hers hazily. It had round windows and a big dressing table with a mirror on it. I have the mirror on my dressing table now. She always had lovely prints and pictures in her bathrooms and a nice chair—that kind of thing.

EMMA BURNS I always say you need to sleep in all of your guest bedrooms and to use all of the bathrooms. I totally agree with the Nancy Lancaster approach to bathrooms. I love bathrooms to be real rooms and have a wonderful window and lovely curtains, and certainly a comfortable chair—also maybe a big rug and flowers and books, pictures, a radio for music . . . the works. However, I will say I love, love, love marble. I adore using interesting marble in bathrooms, but this doesn't mean that they have to be clinical-looking.

LIBBY CAMERON The interpretation of a person, a family, or a house is where each and every project should start and end. Some may think that decorating, as a profession, is frivolous, but helping to make rooms for one to love is worthwhile and important. To be able to transform a bleak space into a room to love is very gratifying. The utmost consideration should always be given to how people live, what their needs are, what will make them feel at peace, and what will constitute a timeless, welcoming, comfortable, and comforting room. Working on the transformation of spaces was, and still is, such a great process—each one is different. But the emphasis always was and always should be comfort.

BEGINNINGS

We found a small farmhouse in Far Hills, a thing of wonder. It was yellow with white shutters, a picket fence, and apple trees all around. Twenty-one and full of confidence, I wasn't the least bit afraid of what people might say about my taste. When the Parishes offered to give us furniture from their town house, I chose a suite of black ebony, covered in Aubusson tapestry. There was a carpet to match, the one the Parish children used to skate over. I then did something no one had ever heard of: I painted the ebony furniture white. Harry's mother would choke before allowing that the effect was "interesting." But I knew what I was after, and I was delighted with the result. Ficus trees stood in the corners of the living room—no one had seen one before. Mattress ticking and damask tablecloths with the Parish crest, which I painted scarlet, were sewn into curtains. Mrs. Parish wondered why I hadn't left the windows bare until the real curtains arrived.

In our bedroom I painted the floor, another daring innovation. I wanted it cherry red with white diamonds, and Harry spent much of the summer on hands and knees, making sure the diamonds came out right. I had the mantel made from structural blocks of Steuben glass applied to the wall, which I had painted red just there. Over the bed taffeta flowed down from a crown. Now of course hangings are something no one can go to sleep without. The first night Harry and I kept the lights on because it was so beautiful.

Some people were horrified by what I'd done. Someone said, "Well, I guess you will always be different, Sister." But I had accomplished something original. I knew it and they knew it. Soon friends came seeking advice. It never occurred to me that I wasn't qualified to give it.

For some reason, I had complete confidence in what I was doing. The furniture arranging came naturally to me. It all seemed obvious. I made some mistakes, of course—you do in almost any house—but the final result was very interesting and very notable.

—SISTER PARISH

PETER DUNHAM HAS USED A VARIETY OF BLUES IN THIS SITTING ROOM. THE SUBTLE PALETTE CREATES A WONDERFUL BACKGROUND FOR THE ECLECTIC MIX OF FURNITURE.

Mita Corsini Bland 2001

FURNITURE PLANS
and BACKGROUND

I always tell people to get the bones of your house right. You can buy furniture until the cows come home, but get the bones right—get the floor plan right, get it to flow. SUZANNE RHEINSTEIN

LIBBY CAMERON I find that the client usually holds the compass when starting a project: they have the information and opinions that lead the way with their preferences for colors and styles—and you really have to pay attention to what they say. How people dress, their clothing and shoes, their jewelry and appearance tells you a lot. What they have in terms of furniture, and how they like their rooms to work, is a beginning cue. I ask a lot of questions, some quite personal really given that I barely know the person—like what size bed do they prefer, do they like to sleep in the dark, do they read or watch television in bed—questions you certainly wouldn't ask the person sitting next to you at a dinner party. But the more you know, the easier it is to begin and to understand which direction to take. There is a confidence that comes with knowledge and with that understanding, you can move forward and create a house that can reflect their dreams.

TODD ROMANO Do you start with the rug or do you finish with the rug? It depends on what kind of rug we are talking about. If we are talking about a fabulous rug that you've got, then we are going to start with that rug. I don't want to have things dictated to me and yet sometimes it's very helpful to have a starting point. It's also a great telling point as to who they are and what they like, so sometimes that doesn't intimidate me. If somebody has something to offer up, I am thrilled—we can start with that.

THE FURNITURE IN A NEW YORK CITY CIRCULAR SITTING ROOM FLOATS IN THE MIDDLE, CREATING AN ARRANGEMENT THAT ENHANCES THE ROOM'S SHAPE.

WILLIAM HODGINS Hopefully the space has some architectural trim. If it doesn't, we would specify it. We have cornice samples for people to look at because when painted white, moldings spark up the darkest, dreariest rooms. Good baseboards are important, nice and high—many people forget about the baseboards. If you have sparkling trim, you can use almost any color on the wall and the room seems brighter.

ALBERT HADLEY I think that in order for a room to really be successful there are two important elements: one is to have a very strong point of view about what it is supposed to look like; and two, to be very conscious of what you choose to go in it. For instance, the Paleys' yellow living room—that room had nothing but beautiful upholstery and all of the furniture was French, so there was continuity to it, there was a peacefulness about that room. I think that is what is lacking in a lot of rooms. There is not a strong point of view about what the end result is going to be. If one has the magic eye, as Sister did, this will always be achieved. She certainly could mix and match, but it wasn't that she brought in things that shouldn't be there.

I am constantly changing things—moving doors. Sister almost fired me many times because she wanted to get in there and just do it, and I wanted to move a door six inches or close up a window. She was terrific because we worked it out together, and most of the time it was fairly successful. There is a time and place for everything.

SUZANNE RHEINSTEIN If it's an old house that has been stripped of its details, of its architectural essence, then the question is, do you want to restore it, or do you want to keep it cleaner and simpler? A house can be like the most beautiful, simple black dress—it can look fabulous with a stunning brooch on it. You can keep the simplicity of the architecture and still bring in some beautiful pieces. If everything is brand new, it's all going to just float away, so you need something to ground it—have just one antique in a room, something that has some soul. If a house does not have any architectural integrity, then you really need to decide how to bring that in, how to give it some soul. If it has low ceilings you need to think vertically—you need to think of curtains that are going to be vertical. If it has low ceilings, don't put everything on a horizontal plane. Rooms need definition. Crown molding is relatively easy to add and inexpensive. My advice is to hire a fabulous architect—I am the biggest advocate of architects; they can bring a lot to the table with their expertise. People oftentimes don't think about how you are going to walk into or through a house, and where you're going to plug in lamps, or where you'll need the switch. That's the level of detail and planning that's important to do with an architect and the client.

JOSIE McCARTHY My whole theory on decorating is that when we start, I tell people it's like the old Chinese proverb: "If you buy the best you only cry once." That doesn't mean the most expensive, but it means the most appropriate, the best thing that your budget can buy, so that you will not feel in five years that you have to throw it away. You want to buy things that will last, that are timeless. I believe in timeless classics, whether it is traditional or modern. Get the backgrounds right also. If you are building a house or remodeling, if you get the backgrounds right, you are not going to have to redo the hardest parts, like changing the shape of the room, the marble, the lighting, the floor. Get that right, from the placement of the plugs to all the little things that make a difference, because you are not going to change that. You can always repaint and redo your furniture but you are not going to change the background.

MARIO BUATTA You need to begin with an architectural sense. When Mrs. Parish took on Albert—that was a dream team. She knew nothing about architecture. I am not mocking her; she had a wonderful sense of making a house a home and making it comfortable and making it cozy, but Albert gave it the architecture, the scale. She used to put little lamps on big tables and she would put big lamps on little tables. It's all out of whack but interesting; it was cozy and nice and it looked like it was always there. That's the way it should be—like a garden—it just continues to grow.

MILES REDD I have a motto that if you get your walls and your floor right, you can stick anything in there. I have a tendency not to be overly regimented in terms of a floor plan. I map one out, but then I always think that great rooms are about what you love and what you are inspired by. A good decorator can get in there and push the furniture around in a way that makes it work and edit out what won't work.

JEFFREY BILHUBER Obviously seating groups help us understand how to use a room. Furnished rooms appear larger than unfurnished. Actually putting more furniture in makes a room more satisfying. You feel you can navigate your way through. You understand scale and proportion and the relative size of rooms from the way that you break it up into smaller, more intimate groups.

You know walking into a house—you get a read before you get out of the car—what should be happening inside that front door. You also get a read of houses that you should never cross the threshold of, ever. I have pulled up to a couple of houses and said, "Just keep driving." Who was it that had that really great story? Was it Rose Cummings? Potential clients told her, "We have wanted to hire you for years, and we just got the new apartment, so would you please come over and take a look and tell us what we should do?" She showed up, and they looked at the living room, the library, the dining room, the pantry; they did a full circle and they ended up back at the front door and said, "I am so glad you are here. Now, what do you think we should do?" "Move and call me when you do. This one is a goner."

TODD ROMANO It's the backgrounds, which to me are always floor, walls, windows, and seating; then you come in and you do all those other layers on top of that. But when we are doing our floor plans I always think about the scale of the furniture—whether it is going to be an Odom chair, whether it is going to be a straight back or a scroll back. Can you see it from the side or does it need to be shoved up against the wall? That will determine which style we will choose, and how high the backs should be and how high the arms should be, as we begin to mix those other things. That's tough for a lot of people. It's especially tough for the novice, going into furniture stores to try to buy furniture nowadays, because the scale is so whacked out. It's so big—it's just wild how big the upholstered furniture is—it's like the McDonald's of furniture. It's like, "Super-size me." We have these wildly overscaled pieces that are available to the public through most furniture stores, and their scale is ghastly. They really don't work in New York apartments. So people who probably are not living in a very big space end up with the sofa that swallows up the whole wall. They never stop to think, is this going to look really big when I get it home? They are lucky if they can just get it through the door.

DAVID WEBSTER We don't live in museums. I always get offended when I walk into someone's house and they say, "No, no, don't sit in that chair." My opinion is if that is the case, then the chair should not be in the room. Furniture has to be comfortable and it has to feel comfortable and look comfortable. You were talking about how Sister loved to see a fire going. Well, there is just nothing better than walking in and seeing cushions plumped up and a fire going. It's just that wonderful cozy feeling.

JEFFREY BILHUBER What we try to do with clients is let them guide the way. Usually we will spend a couple of hours with them in our resource library, letting them go through our fabric samples. We just bring out bins of cloth and say, "Honestly, do not overprocess this. Do not think of this as a pillow, where would it go, or if this were upholstery, where would it go? Just go where your heart tells you to." I will take it to the next step. I usually start with a comfort zone.

PAUL VINCENT WISEMAN You have to go back to the deep, physiological aspects, so that when you're in a room that's well lit, there's a warmth—there's a center. The fireplace is going to disappear in our lifetime because of the pollution, so we are going to have to come up with new ways to create the hearth.

LIBBY CAMERON Flexibility is such an important part of life in general, but especially with a house or a room. Rooms in which conversation can flourish between two or twenty people—rooms in which people feel instantly welcome, comfortable and at ease, where people would rather sit than stand—are rooms that really work. Chairs can be moved around and people shouldn't be afraid of moving furniture or pulling up a bench to join a conversation. Some people are afraid of letting things get out of place and those rooms that are always the same can become stagnant and lifeless. It is all about keeping rooms alive, giving rooms character and personality—a point of view. I like to think that houses have character. Our house certainly does, maybe even too much. It is filled with my animal collection and many different colors, and kids and dogs—it is lively. We can have two or thirty people over, and they spread out between three rooms—the living room, the library, and the dining room, and it works—the house seems to swell surreptitiously. Our children always have their friends over, which I love; their energy and chatter is wonderful, but our kitchen is tiny so our dining room is where they sit and talk. It's a cozy room. Many people have said that our house reflects us, which I take as a compliment. A house should be just that—a reflection of the person or people living in it.

SUZANNE TUCKER In big-scale rooms that are beautifully furnished, the challenge is to make them welcoming. People stand at the door and say, "Oh, isn't this a beautiful room?" but they are not drawn into it. The way you achieve this is by thinking in terms of creating intimacy in a big room. There again, focusing on seating groups is the key to that success. With the biggest rooms that I have done, I've made them feel intimate by doing just that—creating multiple seating groups.

MARIO BUATTA I remember reading about Sister Parish, about how she could walk into a room and place a sofa. It's what you do—it's a given.

THIS VIBRANT VINY WALLPAPER CREATES A COLORFUL CHINOISERIE-INSPIRED BACKDROP FOR FURNITURE AND ART.

Mita Corsini Bland

Eventually your eye is trained so you know exactly where things can go—the average layperson doesn't. So they say, "Oh my God, she's a genius—she knows where to put the sofa." It's true because they've never thought about it.

PETER DUNHAM Once we are over where the TV goes, which is obviously the most important thing in decorating, bar none, then you can start building your furniture plan. Soon after you have to have a little click, and that is where the interest comes from.

TODD ROMANO I love doing floor plans. My favorite thing is getting the plans back from the draftsman. I roll my tissue paper out on them and I start sketching out different ways to arrange furniture. We usually do three, four, five, six different ways, then I will whittle that down to the two or three best ways to do the room. Sometimes the architecture will dictate the layout; sometimes there is only one way to do it. I love multiple seating arrangements—there is something a little old-fashioned about that. It goes back to the days of Mrs. Parish and the Paleys, and people entertaining on a more formal scale—a grander scale. I try not to overfurnish rooms. I was reading the Billy Baldwin book when I was twelve years old; my mother had it. I remember him saying, "Look at your room after you have had a party, the day after, before you clean up and straighten up, and you will see that people will have moved the furniture, if it is not arranged that way already. They will have moved it into little circles and groups for conversation." That has always stayed with me and I love that concept. So on the one hand I am a big proponent of that and I love the idea of what I call the "wagon wheel complex"—that you have some sort of a circle or an ability to make a circle for conversation, where you can pull chairs up, because really, that's what people like to do at parties. I do love multiple seating groups but again the size of the room dictates the number of groups you can have. If you have one room that is not particularly grand in proportion, it's a little silly to try to make it something it's not.

BUNNY WILLIAMS Everybody instinctively puts the furniture around the room—the outside of the room—they don't know how to use the inside space. Today frankly there is so much written about floor plans. You can't open a magazine without somebody doing a floor plan and people who are going to do it themselves need to pay some attention. I think today more than ever that there are incredible sources for self-help in design. Magazines like *Domino* or *House Beautiful*—they are all trying to teach the layperson how to do it.

EMMA BURNS I always start with a room layout, because I think a room has to be organized. You can't of course create a room which is perfect for everything, so you have to understand its main uses. Obviously, rooms have to be as flexible as possible. Another reason for doing floor plans is to see how, if you are going to have more people, you can bring in an extra piece without destroying the feeling of the room. I like to look and see what existing furniture they have got and if there are pieces we can use; whether we are going to recover existing upholstery or whether we are going to make new sofas and armchairs. Then we need to know if we are going to have shapes, which are modern, or if there is going to be something like an antique piece that we can copy, and have a pair of something.

PAUL VINCENT WISEMAN I do a preliminary floor plan and then I have them walk through it with me to critique it. This is what I think works: I say tell me about how you really live. We redline it—it's very rough—and then we put it on real paper and they get to think about it more. But I make them walk through and we talk about everything. How does it look, how does it function?

BUNNY WILLIAMS A floor plan is so important. I do it on paper; I scale it on paper. I think that you should then try and scale it on the elevations. We are lucky we have all the drawings so we can do that. I think if people don't have it, they can make a template on the floor to really see how big that chair is that can work. They will be surprised. A lot of commercial upholstery is huge. I think the biggest mistake most people make is scale; it is very hard for people to get the scale right. Things are often too small or too big, or something is too small and then something else is too big. It just drives you crazy. I don't think that is something that you can learn—it is instinctive. Sister Parish had the best sense; she never looked at a floor plan. I think I really understood it when I learned to draw, because you learn to see proportions, so you can walk into a room and know that this cabinet needs to be ten feet tall and six feet wide—you just know it. Scale makes or breaks a room. A really interesting room has things at different scale. You anchor a room with your bigger things, and then fill in with smaller pieces. There is a balance when it's done—there is a real harmony to it. That's why I end up really working on every floor plan of every job we do, because as good as people are, it takes a long time to begin to know that that chair is going to look perfect next to that table.

DANIEL ROMUALDEZ I think it depends on the style of the room. With a modern room one tends to want a very clean line and just to have one exclamation point. It's like modern architecture: you will see a horizontal line and one vertical. In a more traditional room you want to mix it up. I try to balance that out with each room.

LIBBY CAMERON I hang paintings and use furniture carefully, so that every thing isn't at the same height, so that your eye goes up and down around the room. I think it's very important that everything in the room not be the same height, that there not be a waterline around a room. Skylines are created in rooms by the use of furniture, art, and curtains. I think that is one of the most important elements of a room to consider—creating a rolling horizontal line that takes your eye around a room.

MARTHA ANGUS I have a double ceiling in my own house in Napa. It's this cube that is 26 feet square by 26 feet high and I have all of this furniture. I

noticed there was a waterline around the room. Then I found these panels that were 13 or 14 feet high. I had seen a picture of them and knew I had to have those. What's wonderful about them is that they take your eye halfway up the wall so you don't have a waterline.

PETER DUNHAM I think that's a very important part of decorating that amateurs don't really get, the idea that you can't have everything at the same height.

MURALS ADD INTEREST, AND CAN ADD HEIGHT TO A ROOM. THE TREES IN THIS MURAL MAKE THE CEILING FEEL HIGHER; THE SWAGS AND JABOTS AT THE WINDOWS ALSO ADD TO THE ILLUSION OF HEIGHT.

SUITABILITY

I think anything that aesthetically takes a project off-key is inappropriate. Let's say one can have their own sense of appropriateness, and so you don't have to stick to a very strict script necessarily. You can get out of the box, and I think that's the magic of it all—when one is able to get out of the box and still stay in the same room.   ALBERT HADLEY

LIBBY CAMERON   The editing process of a job is so important; that is one of the wonderful things that Albert Hadley and Sister Parish taught me. Once a scheme had been approved by a client, we would begin to fine-tune the entire room and figure what worked, what didn't, and what would be a better alternative. To this day, I have moments when a room comes to mind, and suddenly I have a thought about what might be better and make notes to remind myself to make the change when I get back to the office. When a room really evolves and becomes clear, there can be elements that don't feel right—the balance can feel off, or a table may feel better in another place—and that is where the editing process is so important. The layers come afterward and are what make the difference, in both lifting your eyes and creating a skyline, and by the inclusion of many textures. Not everything works—consistency and continuity are very important—you can't just add a random piece and expect the aesthetic to hold. Not everyone understands that, and understanding it is important. All of the elements of a room are a part of a whole, and it is so important to not lose sight of that.

MARIO BUATTA   The young decorators haven't got a clue. It can be the rug that is the wrong size—not only the size of the furniture—the color of the room,

PAUL WISEMAN DESIGNED THE LIBRARY IN THIS 1950S MAYBECK-STYLE HOUSE IN MARIN COUNTY. WISEMAN CAPITALIZED ON THE SLIGHT ASIAN UNDERCURRENT AND DRAMATIC SCALE THAT ALLOWED THE CLIENT'S ECLECTIC TASTES TO SUCCESSFULLY COEXIST WITH THE ARCHITECTURE.

the windows—anything. Let's say you have windows that are in the wrong place and then you put bright fabrics on them or patterns, or something that points out the defects in the room. If you have a room that's blue and you have a window here and a window here and no window there, make all the window curtains blue so it looks more uniform. They don't think of it, but the biggest mistake is scale. People never understand how big this should be or how little that should be. They don't get it. Everything is set up the way they see it in the shop. That's how some people's houses look; they see it in the shops and in the magazines and that's the way they live.

PAUL VINCENT WISEMAN I tell my clients just because you can afford to have your ceiling look like a runway strip at a jet airport doesn't mean you should. When do you stop? Where, at what juncture is it enough?

ALBERT HADLEY Well, that's suitability. I think a lot of people want expensive-looking interiors. I may think that's totally inappropriate for the person, but you can't always tell that to the client. Having something because it's wildly expensive doesn't make it good. That's where we come to a rather diplomatic situation in which you have to be strong about what you consider to be the best solution for the project. Another thing that I find is somewhat lacking—not just in people in my office, but in other young people that I talk to—is a decisiveness about what they think is really the best option, and a tendency to confuse the client with too many options. I like the client to have no options, frankly. To start with, I like to say, "This is our plan, this is what we think," then if something comes up and for some reason they don't like it, you have a backup plan. But you don't present anything that's a backup at first; you have to be definite and you have to be enthusiastic.

LIBBY CAMERON What about the "shoulds" and "shouldn'ts"? There are some "should nots" that I know—you taught me that, Albert. I try always to be careful, to be firm yet gentle with people about why I think what I do and why something feels right or not. It all has to work together, it has to feel right—

nothing in a room should swear at anything else. My instinct sways me on which way to go. It's always a challenge to put my foot down with a client, but when I know they are asking for something that is just out of place or wrong, I get a surge of conviction. It's really a matter of editing.

ALBERT HADLEY I think that it's probably through experience that one knows what works and what does not, what looks right and what doesn't look right. I think that you and I today really break a lot of the rules.

CAROLYN ENGLEFIELD We often imagine that our taste level or choices have to measure up. But as a matter of fact, they really don't because it is all relative to one's frame of reference, education, and exposure. In a way, I really think that there is no right or wrong because taste, like art and personal opinion, is so subjective. Being and living in the moment is what counts and makes the difference.

JEFFREY BILHUBER I think cohesiveness is really the key to success. I know clearly that with this house that I am building, a late nineteenth-century, 1860s, Greek revival house, there is no getting around it outside of tearing the house down, which is what most people would have done. In fact, that is probably why it just sat there, because no one could solve the riddle of it

ALBERT HADLEY'S REDESIGN OF NELSON ROCKEFELLER'S FIFTH AVENUE APARTMENT INCORPORATED MANY OF THE DETAILS FROM THE ORIGINAL DESIGN BY THE MODERNIST JEAN MICHEL FRANK.

and they didn't want to take on such a daunting project. I feel like I am the custodian of this house; I have been allowed to give it life. The last two people that looked at the house made it very clear they were simply going to take the house down. It gave me more reason and more motivation to save the spirit of this house.

JOHN ROSSELLI So many people make the mistake of interpretation and falter on what is appropriate. They move to the tropics and think they have to have a tropical house—just because it is a tropical house doesn't mean that it has to look like a tropical house. They get carried away.

A very funny story: I went to see my urologist/proctologist the other day; he is very nice. Then all of a sudden after the examination, he closed the door and said, "Can I ask you a personal question?" That's the last thing you want your doctor to say to you—that kind of doctor anyway. I said, "Certainly," and he said, "I want to show you my blueprints." I really started laughing—he said do you mind if I ask you a personal question—how much more personal could we get?

He had just built a house in Phoenix somewhere and has this big house here in Greenwich, and it's all filled with antiques, very pretty. He said my wife and I don't know what to do with it. I said, "First of all, there is no reason you can't take some of your antiques." I asked what kind of carpets they had. He said mostly oriental carpets so I asked, "Are they those fussy red and blue ones?" He said, "No, no, they are geometric patterns." "Well," I said, "they are just as good as Indian carpets so there is no reason why you can't use some of these things. Surround yourself with things you're comfortable with, things you have lived your whole life with."

TELEVISIONS, GOOD HOUSEKEEPING, and OTHER PRIORITIES

Televisions don't bother me. I hate all this fussy TV business. I hate those things that pop up from the foot of the bed—they look like caskets. I like them behind mirrors, or even in a bedroom over a fireplace. I have been using a lot of flat-screen TVs and hanging paintings over them. MARIO BUATTA

LIBBY CAMERON I worked on an apartment in New York City, and there was a flat-screen TV. It looked so just there, so austere, that we decided to put it behind something—to find something really fun and interesting to put in front of it. The TV was in a family room, next to the living room, so the two rooms had to complement each other. I had a box made to go around it—it opens like a cabinet, behind the doors is the television. The box frame is silver leaf, stepped, almost Art Deco in feel, and in the center of the front is a big red apple—it's a very visually strong element in the room. It's whimsical but treated in a somewhat serious way, although the apple is quite playful really.

BRIAN McCARTHY We have clients with seventeen or eighteen televisions in a house—it depends. At the end of the day when you're tired, you gravitate toward the TV; you don't really feel like talking. In some cases I don't mind seeing a TV out, but it depends how it's placed and where it's placed. Sometimes it's fine mounted on the wall; in other cases it's fine on top of a piece of furniture, but sometimes you really want it hidden behind doors. Think about the television in terms of the practicality, of where it is—you don't want to always be opening and closing doors. If the doors are going to stand open all the time, it's not going to be very attractive. You're better off putting it in a bookcase where it will be set within books and objects, and let it become part

of the composition. TVs are a problem. More and more people want them, and they want them to be big.

SUSAN BARTLETT CRATER Televisions can also make a room feel more human. Remember my grandmother's library with that old TV with the rabbit ears antenna coming up? This is where people sat when she had them over for tea or drinks, and the TV was on a trolley table that moved around. It was just there—it was a part of the room.

JANE CHURCHILL I don't hide them. I think those modern sleek ones are great—they look so nice. I wouldn't have one in my living room because I wouldn't watch it in there. I have a huge one in our bedroom. I really hate them under tablecloths. I don't mind them in cupboards.

DANIEL ROMUALDEZ It is really hard to decorate around a TV, but I try my best because I love watching it. I think if the room is well decorated and beautiful enough, the TV is just another element. It is harder in the really minimalist rooms without it looking like a cliché flat screen on the wall. I ask clients, how much TV do you actually watch? If you are only going to watch it when there is an earthquake in China or there is an election, then you can hide it. But if it's the first thing you do when you get up or it's the first thing you do when you get home, and it's on the whole time you are there, then there is no point in hiding it. I try and position it so it's not the first thing you see when you walk into the room, for instance, on the door side of the room. You come in and you see the pretty room, and then the TV. I remember seeing the Brandolini house in Venice; he had a TV on an amazing console with a beautiful lamp on either side. There was the TV—right there—and it just all of a sudden fit in.

A VIGNETTE IN A ROOM DONE BY JEFFREY BILHUBER COMBINES A WONDERFUL MIXTURE OF BASKETS AND DIFFERENT TYPES OF FURNITURE—A WICKER CHAIR COMBINED WITH MORE IMPORTANT ANTIQUES AND OBJECTS. THE INFORMAL SIMPLICITY AND THE TULIPS BRIGHTEN ALL OF THE OBJECTS.

TODD ROMANO I grew up with an emphasis on good housekeeping. That is also something that is very Southern—polished floors, polished silver, starched linens, simple, good food. Hospitality. So I come to this business with that as my background and that really is my love. To me that is what I see lacking in a lot of these houses. When I get up on a Sunday if I am in town and I am staying in, I will make the bed up and then I will turn the sheets down a little. Then I will get back into bed—when it is somewhat fresh—with the newspapers after I have taken my dogs for a walk. But it is still sort of made. As children, we had to take our dishes to the sink or the pantry. We had responsibilities. We all would be corralled into doing yard work, which I hated as a kid but love as an adult.

BUNNY WILLIAMS A house has to be taken care of and people have to be honest about their help: do they have it or do they not have it. Because otherwise, what is going to happen to this place? The maintenance of it is huge. It's less than a garden but it's still a lot. You know, a house that is tidied up and put together can look fantastic, where that same house that is in chaos can look horrible.

CAROLYN ENGLEFIELD I believe many decorators have this desire to constantly improve the way they and their clients live. I recognize that it is their passion and compulsion to constantly create solutions, solve problems, fulfill their client's dreams and desires, as well as to shop until they drop, in an effort to educate their clients about a better way of living. It is their life's mission to be creating a nest, a refuge, a retreat—a special place for living.

What could be nicer than a pretty vase of fresh flowers to make a room come alive? It is the simple pleasures that make life more enjoyable. It is not all just about the decorating—it is more about how a place looks and feels to be in. When I am scouting for Veranda, I know right away when I see it if it is right for us, because I understand it, I love it, I can taste it, I can smell it, but most of all, I can feel it. It is not so much about the cost or quantity of things, but more about the quality of life that makes it worth living.

AN APPLE PRINT HAS
BEEN CUT IN HALF AND
MOUNTED IN THE DOORS
OF A STEPPED BOX
THAT HAS A SILVER LEAF
FINISH. A FLAT-SCREEN
TELEVISION IS HIDDEN
BEHIND THE DOORS.

SUSAN BARTLETT CRATER The two things that stood out—if you knew Sister's rooms—were the housekeeping and the flowers. They were both incredibly important to her and she was a genius at having the people who helped her successfully implement her likes and dislikes. One of her favorite housekeepers in Maine, Wilamena, was known to lift up Sister's canopy bed with a car jack to make sure she successfully vacuumed the ancient rug underneath. As she said a million times, she never went to bed before making sure everything was in its place. The thing about good housekeeping, which she understood very well, is that it is really a cornerstone of luxury and comfort, which ultimately doesn't exist if a house is unkempt. So the slate she started with was always bright and shiny and it stayed that way. She respected people who took care of their houses.

Another part of housekeeping she focused on was making it convenient and well-organized. She was a fanatic about having well-placed and large linen and broom closets. She was also a fanatic about having sharpened pencils and "Don't Forget" pads next to every phone, beautifully laundered linens, highly polished floors (and shoes), magnificently organized closets, luxurious puffed-up pillows, sturdy old baskets filled with firewood next to the fireplace, and lots and lots of flowers everywhere. The flowers were as natural as she could get them. She preferred bulbs and masses of anything wild and unpretentious or something more sophisticated for the city. She told us a house was not complete without flowers.

BRIAN McCARTHY The organization of closets and the basic functionality, not of what you see but what's behind doors, is key. The organization of kitchens, bathrooms, mudrooms, and butler's pantries, flower rooms—whatever, depending upon the kind of house it is and the lifestyle—is always really important. Some people don't have the luxury of space so you have to be very clever and efficient in coming up with solutions for storing things. It can be as simple as a draped table and under that draped table I have all my Christmas ornaments. We all know the Container Store and all these companies that do all of these storage things that go under beds. I don't like that because I don't like the idea that it's just going to collect dust, but we have to be practical that way.

We work with a lot of consultants in developing how things are laid out. It can be as easy as a lot of adjustable shelves. Wouldn't you rather have ten adjustable shelves rather than five, so that you're not reaching through a stack that's 18 inches high of sweaters to get to the bottom of a color? You pull something out and everything topples over. You are better off having three shelves for the 18 inches and having 6-inch stacks so you can really pull things out easily. The same thing applies in a kitchen. Instead of having two sets of china that are stacked on top of each other, add another shelf to break the space up and make things easy to access, because if you can't access it you're not going to use it. If you don't see it in your closet, you're never going to wear it, so why have it?

Housekeeping is so important. When I have a big dinner party, I want to come in to a clean kitchen the next morning. I do not want to come in and see a pile of plates in the sink. I want to come in and it's a new day—yesterday was yesterday and it's a new day. The way a house is organized contributes to the ease of housekeeping. For example, with a sofa, do you want to have to go and fluff up fifteen pillows? That's a lifestyle question.

I remember being in Dark Harbor with Mrs. Parish. After dinner, the two of us went around fluffing up all the pillows. We had a really good laugh over that because we both just instinctively did it.

THE NATURAL FLOWERS IN CLAY POTS ADD A BURST OF COLOR AND CASUAL WARMTH TO THIS LIVING ROOM.

SUZANNE RHEINSTEIN I am a big believer that even in the most formal architecture, if you can't kick off your Manolo's after a dinner party and throw your feet up on the sofa, you're not living. That's where Americans have gone astray. They take this, "Oh, it's this formal room" approach versus just living in your house.

TODD ROMANO You know, Mario always talks about how a house is like a garden—nothing stays the same. That tree outside the window will be different next year. I love that. I like whimsy and unusual mixtures and the layering of patterns and different things. I always look for things that have some sort of pizzazz or a little zip to them, or a little something that adds an extra touch, that keeps a room from being too perfect or studied. In fact I almost like things if they are a little bit wrong. We have been so fortunate, we have been exposed to such great things, we all had great training, we all got to work for great people, and we have been in and out of beautiful houses. But I think the really special houses are the ones that possess a little bit of all of those qualities, whether it is personal touches, personal mementos—maybe even one chair that is a little bit worn out. But most important, people have to feel comfortable in these houses and need to enjoy living in them.

ELEMENTS

When Robert Frost spoke at John F. Kennedy's Inauguration, he said that he had just come from "a temple on the North Shore." Frost was referring to a house in Manchester-by-the-Sea, where my great-aunt Mrs. Thomas Jefferson Coolidge lived. Coolidge Point was on a peninsula of land surrounded by the Atlantic on three sides. Originally, a large formidable brick house stood there on the point, designed by McKim, Mead and White, but it was torn down. The Coolidges hired Page Cross and Mrs. Parish to help build a new house. It was completely different from the original house; its façade was a whitewashed brick, it was low and looked quite casual and unassuming as you drove into the courtyard. When I was a child, we stayed in the "Farmhouse" near Auntie Catherine's house on Coolidge Point at the beginning of each summer on our way to Maine. The driveway was lined with huge rhododendron bushes. I can still remember the smells of the flowering bushes and of the low-tide mudflats in Kettle Cove.

Architecturally, the house was very clean and balanced, and bowed to the natural beauty of the setting, angled toward the sea. There was a small rotunda as you entered the house, which must have been a nod to Thomas Jefferson; it had Gilbert Stuart's portraits of the first five presidents hanging on the walls and nothing else; there wasn't a table, or any lamps or rugs—just a small fireplace straight ahead in the center. The floor was a beige marble with square dots, and there were hallways that stretched to the right and to the left; there were no other rooms that one's eye could see, just angled doors and perpendicular hallways. It was grand, but its grandeur wasn't intimidating; it was light and bright and this perhaps sounds strange, but the architectural perfection of that entrance, and the softness of the materials and of the colors made it very welcoming; the smell of flowers and salt air drew you in.

Behind and to the right of the rotunda was a large living room, in tones of peach, with a beautiful big fireplace mantel. The floor was pickled and painted

THE BLACK WALLS IN DANIEL ROMUALDEZ'S LIBRARY PROVIDE A WONDERFUL BACKGROUND FOR THE COLORS IN THE BRIGHT RUG AND THE BOOKS.

in a circular pattern, using tones of beige and cream. There were two large seating groups, one by the fireplace and one in the bay window and there were two painted French cabinets with wire-front doors on either side of the opening into the sun room. The room was serene and inviting, warm and cozy, and very luxurious. The ceilings were very high and the chandelier in the center brought your eye down. The windows were big and looked out over the point. At the water's edge there was a huge urn, much taller than I was as a young child. The urn was framed in the bay window opposite the fireplace as you looked out at the sea. The sun room beyond the living room had trompe l'oeil bamboo lattice walls, creamy white rattan furniture covered in a hand-blocked fabric with big pale yellow and beige sunflowers. There was a thread that connected these two rooms—the sun room was an extension of the living room in terms of the palette; the ceiling was a pale melon color. There was a sun-kissed, bleached tone to both rooms, yet the materials, the rugs and luxurious upholstery in the living room, were much more grand than the rattan and straw rugs in the sun room. Both rooms were very welcoming and they melded into the other.

Across the hall, there was a wonderful, quite small library, with bright red carpeting and a small loveseat and chairs by the fireplace. Auntie Catherine's husband, Jeff Coolidge, was a descendant of Thomas Jefferson; his desk was tucked in the bay window at the far end of the room. Auntie Catherine always sat at that desk: I remember entering that room and seeing her sitting there, her eyeglasses slipping down the bridge of her nose. The telephone was on a little table on the side of the desk closer to the window and had phone books, pads of paper, and a pretty pencil cup made with Italian paper. Jefferson's ink well was on the desk along with a lovely magnifying glass that had an ivory handle and a worn brass letter opener. In a cabinet hanging on the wall were Jefferson's eyeglasses and shoe buckles and some of the buttons from his military jacket. Auntie Catherine always giggled at me when I tried on his eyeglasses.

The dining room was at the other end of the house and also had a beautiful view of the point. It was a wonderful, glazed melon color and had a very pretty marble mantel with a design of concentric, overlapping circles, a detail that Page Cross repeated on the glass French doors used at the entrance to the room.

The furniture was mostly painted faux bamboo, the table an oval, painted in pale tones anchored by a pale, soft Oushak rug. There was a silver leaf, tall three-panel screen that stood in the corner, which added height to the room and a shimmer of elegance.

The house was always filled with beautiful flowers. Bruno was in charge of her greenhouse, which was beyond the dining room side of the house. Bruno lived in a lovely, old brick house that was attached to the greenhouse; it was the only one of the original buildings that remained. He was a kind and gentle man, who whistled and hummed as he worked—he had the loveliest smile. Auntie Catherine's little dog Brenda followed him everywhere. Bruno's passion was his greenhouse, and flowers were his life. He contributed so much to the feel of the house, to the elegance and warmth it had.

Auntie Catherine's house had all of the elements of an elegant house—it was a reflection of her. She was beautiful and very elegant, and always so gentle and welcoming. She had that wonderful ability to make you feel like you were the most important person in the world. The different elements of this house on Coolidge Point combined to make it a house that everyone loved to visit. It welcomed you, it drew you in—it was comfortable and luxurious and serene.

—LIBBY CAMERON

DRESSING
the WINDOW

John Fowler influenced all of the decorators—Nancy Lancaster and even Mrs. Henry Parish—they learned to really understand and appreciate elaborate curtains. I think some of them were and are absolutely beautiful. I think it's important to know how to do that, in its place. ALBERT HADLEY

LIBBY CAMERON I find that I use valances quite a lot on windows, without curtain panels—just to articulate the window. I like light, and it is a way to accentuate the window and add a dimension to a space. Curtains definitely soften a room, although it depends on the space. If the ceiling is low, a valance at the window will bring your eye down, and create an unsettling visual line—a waterline, in which case poles and rings may be the better solution. Dressing a window has to be appropriate to the room. If you don't know what to do, sometimes less is better.

I have the tin valances that were made for the windows of the guest room I did at the Kips Bay Show House when I was at Parish-Hadley. They were made by an auto body shop and painted by the artist Chuck Fisher. They are rounded at the ends and have a painted contrast edging and heading. I love them. That was the one thing Mrs. Parish and Albert were always insistent about—that everything had to have a finished edge. The details were essential to them both, and the details had to be subtle. Albert preferred a ¼-inch contrast binding or a ¼-inch self-bias edge, and Mrs. Parish liked braids and the cotton fringes and tapes that Colefax used to make. I remember going to an upholstery shop with Mrs. Parish right after I had started working for her. She walked in and all of the upholstered pieces had been brought out onto the floor for her to see. She

THE PROPORTION OF THE BEAUTIFUL CURTAINS IN THIS FORMER ARTIST'S STUDIO IN SOUTHAMPTON, NEW YORK, ENHANCES THE GRANDEUR OF THE ROOM.

said immediately and quite emphatically, "Take all of that hideous wool braid off right this minute." She was quite scary, but she knew it was not right and that the trimming was too heavy and fuzzy for the chintz it was on. Needless to say, it was replaced with something more suitable.

EMMA BURNS It is about attention to detail, absolutely, attention to detail at absolutely every single point—whether it is to a letter that is sent out: how it's laid out, how it's addressed, the placement of the stamp. I mean real attention to detail, because if you can't get the basics of writing a letter right, how can you accomplish anything else?

ALBERT HADLEY Recently I ran into someone that I had worked for years ago. She had just been with Tony Marshall in his mother, Brooke Astor's, apartment. She said she had remarked to Tony, "This is the most beautiful library I have ever seen," about her red library. I said, "Thank you very much." That room reminds me of a curtain story. Because of the structure of the background, there was no reason to have hanging curtains. We had made what are called balloon shades, but I make them in such a way that they don't balloon; they kind of fold up, gracefully. In that room they were very light and they were right against the glass. In Brooke's dining room the curtains were a different story—Brooke wanted "ballroom" curtains. I thought, "Okay, that means 'whoopsy,'" so we made curtains out of green faille silk with pink detailing and overlays. They were very elaborate on the two windows at the end of the room, but they were totally appropriate because there was no view. The curtains just framed the windows. We painted the walls, making them a deeper color, so her beautiful decorative panels would stand out.

In contrast, on the top floor of the Whitneys' town house, one whole side of the room was glass. Betsey and Sis were talking about what they were going to

A BEAUTIFULLY CARVED DOOR CASING FRAMES THE ENTRANCE TO A DINING ROOM IN A TOWN HOUSE DESIGNED BY MOTT B. SCHMIDT. THE CURTAIN VALANCES OF STRIPED SILK ABOVE THE GREEN CURTAIN PANELS FRAME THE WINDOWS AND ALLOW LIGHT INTO THE ROOM.

do; Sis had an idea about lots of curtains since it looked right across the street into another building—there was nothing you wanted to see. I spoke up and I said, "Well, now look, ladies, I think those should be shutters," and Betsey went into a tizzy. We left there and within two days, Sis came back. She had already found the damn shutters. They had to be adjusted a little but they had been painted and she loved them the way they looked. They were almost in a natural pine finish—very pretty and appropriate. She gave up her curtains right away.

If the windows don't bring in a lot of light, I am inclined to use some kind of window covering; it could be strong or not so strong, for instance a blind. I like using the aluminum blinds where it is suitable because they reflect light, and I also like the wonderful woven shades that let light come through, like the old wood shades only more elaborate—I am sure you have all seen them. Now there are these wonderful glass matchsticks—they are marvelous when you don't have a view. The light comes in, and at night the light from the inside illuminates the window—the window covering has a reflective quality yet still lets light come in.

LIBBY CAMERON When I first started at Parish-Hadley, Mrs. Parish told me she only used four valance designs when she first began. I saw some of the most beautiful curtain designs come out of that office. It's hard to believe that she had such a small repertoire at first.

ALBERT HADLEY She did, more or less. I think I have the sketches somewhere in little scrapbooks at the office. Her upholsterer would go with her on a job, and she would decide on a valance design; then she and the upholsterer would work out the scale and length and the details. As time went by and she got more into it, she became more creative. Personally, I like to keep curtains as simple as possible and as architectural as possible. That doesn't mean that they can't have some flair or have some detail, but I think in most architectural situations today, the simpler the better—we want to let the light come in. We want to have a sense of privacy, but a window is a window to do what it's supposed to do. If you can frame it attractively and make it softer, fine, everything in its place.

EMMA BURNS I really like curtains on poles. I like curtains to be as simple as possible because I think that too much fabric can be overwhelming. Again, it depends on the window. If you are doing curtains for a very important room, obviously you would want to design something that would be completely appropriate. If it was a regular house, I would prefer straight curtains hanging on a pole and maybe a shade behind to hide any dead light and to make the windows look taller. This window and curtain thing is like a person—the taller and thinner they are, the better. I always, always contrast-line my curtains so that they are beautiful from the outside and have symmetry from the outside. I like the binding to be very fine, and I like them to break 1½ inches on the floor and not to be heavily lined. If they have to be interlined, I like to use a really thick damask which keeps the fluidity; I hate them to look filtered and sort of over-important. Often the excitement you get from fabric is when you pull it up and it drapes, so you don't want to lose that lovely fluidity or that sort of spontaneity of the fabric. This happens when a curtain maker uses a heavy interlining and the fabric becomes too stiff. I work really closely with the curtain makers and talk with them; I also go down to see the curtains as they are being made.

A STONE VALANCE HAS A CASUAL FORMALITY.

MARIO BUATTA Oh, I love pretty curtains and love dressing windows. I hate plain curtains unless the room calls for it. Normally, I do curtains; there is a reason for them—they keep the chill out. Sometimes pretty curtains are the only architecture in the room and the only thing in the room that draws your attention—not glaringly so, but it is something that is there, that looks pretty.

SUSAN BARTLETT CRATER When I think of the curtains in Parish-Hadley houses, I think of wonderful full curtains with beautiful linings and fantastic trims that were very finished looking. Sister hated anything that was, in her words, "wispy." She didn't like wispy curtains, wispy people, wispy anything. She used rickrack trim in simple Maine houses and beautiful glass beads on curtains in New York. Because she loved fabric, her curtains were a way for her to emphasize it in a room. There were beautiful bed hangings on the canopy beds in all of her houses; they were really another form of curtain in the room. I would not call her curtains overly elaborate, but they were of such high workmanship that they were always a thing of beauty. She spent a lot of time in the workrooms overseeing the work and took great pleasure in the amazing creations that came out of them.

GATHERED FABRIC ON
A POLE IS KNOWN AS A
"SLINKY" HEADING.

Later, on arrival at the workroom, I find the curtains and valances are hanging waiting to be packed. I begin to wonder, is the fringe deep enough? Is the tape set back enough? Could the valance stand more bells? My eye goes to the curtains for the master bedroom. I can't help smiling they are so beautiful. The bed stands alone, and even against the dreary workroom walls with bare lightbulbs, it demands a look of wonder. The canopy is a dome, made like the most beautiful parasol, the pale green fluted posts justify holding the miracle of white muslin bound in grosgrain ribbons, with magic workmanship. The folds meet the center like a star, each point standing alone. One wonders, who could help but sleep.

—SISTER PARISH

DANIEL ROMUALDEZ One of my favorite things is unlined taffeta curtains. They have that luxurious Old World quality yet they look quite modern. For rooms without great proportions, we make very simple curtains. If we have the good fortune to work in a room with amazing height we go for it—we do old-fashioned elaborate curtains. I love to do that. I have made a few pairs of beautiful curtains but I am hankering to design more.

CATHY KINCAID I think the simpler the draperies, the better. Get your dressmaker details in the draperies—pretty pleats at the top. Use beautiful antique finials or antique rings or Robert Kime's hardware, which are the best reproductions I know of for rings and finials. Maybe you don't always put fringe on it—you can get stuck into thinking that you have to have fringe. Do a border using the stripe in a fabric or the border design in a fabric, and run that down the leading edges of the draperies; use the borders in a fabric for the valances.

BUNNY WILLIAMS I will never forget one time making a pair of curtains out of a printed fabric for a very big window. It looked pretty when the curtains were open, but the minute you closed them the entire wall was a print. It would have been one thing if the walls and the curtains had all been the same. From that day on I have never made curtains like that for a big window—unless the room has the same fabric as the curtains. It looks pretty when it is framing the window but if you draw them, you have this whole wall of big pattern and it's not anyplace else. I might do that if I am upholstering a room or putting the same fabric on the wall, but only in that way. Now when I have a big window to work with, I tend to make curtains in the color of the walls, or even a little bit lighter, so at least if the curtains are closed, it's not so busy. But that was a mistake that turned out to be something good—I learned a lesson.

LIBBY CAMERON So many of the little prints have disappeared, which is one of the reasons Susan and I started our fabric company. Everything was white, beige, or graphically bold. I love small prints and use them both as curtains and for curtain lining. They have character, are subtle, and can add texture as curtains and interest, and set off the window in a calming way. When Susan and I started Sister Parish Design, all of our first patterns were small patterns—we are still adding small-scaled prints.

BRIAN McCARTHY I like curtains to break on the floor, so you feel the weight of the curtains, but I don't like 2 inches on the floor. From a housekeeping standpoint, every time I walk into a client's house where I have done curtains that are an inch on the floor, I am forever going around to every curtain and trying to fix it, or to retrain the staff on how to dress curtains and shades—even though it is very simple. I don't like fancy curtains. I like beautifully made curtains with simple details.

DANIEL ROMUALDEZ I agree with you. Today either the valances are over the top and you do very simple curtains, or no valances, then you can do very voluminous curtains with nothing on top. If you do both, clients say, "Oh, it reminds me of my grandmother."

MIRRORS and HANGING ART

When you are hanging a painting, a drawing—different things, when you look at the wall—the arrangement has to be balanced; there has to be a pattern that makes sense. BUNNY WILLIAMS

EMMA BURNS I think we each have a way of hanging pictures. I mean I would think nothing of hanging a beautiful oil painting in a bathroom. That wouldn't faze me at all, or in a kitchen. I would hang it there because I thought it was so beautiful and wonderful, and it would give me huge pleasure every time I was in that room. I wouldn't think, it's a fantastic painting therefore it's got to be in a special place. I would have a bit of irreverence about things and how they are used. I would just use them because they are a great shape and they do the job for me.

Roger Banks, who I worked for here, would frame a sheet of second-class stamps because they were the most beautiful blue. They were on the table propped up on a little easel or something, and he decided that they would look great as a fantastic piece of art. I learned from him that you could play with those different things, put them together, and that one thing makes the other thing sing.

BUNNY WILLIAMS Paintings shouldn't be too high. I think that if you are in a hall they can be higher because you are standing. In a living room where I am sitting, I tend to hang them a little bit lower. I think that pictures that aren't hung with a theme are sometimes more interesting because it looks more collected. To start, I lay it all out on the floor to see; if you have a big picture, then maybe you have two small ones or however you are going to balance it. I don't think they have to have a theme—I don't think they have to be all oil paintings. I think you can do oils and drawings and use something modern with something traditional.

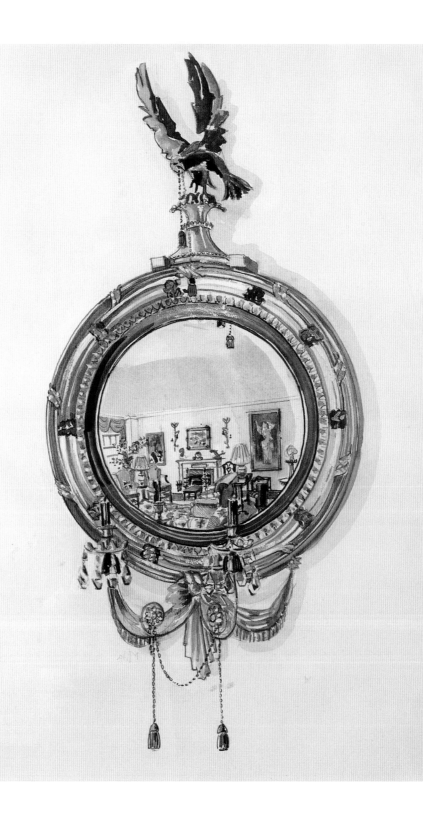

I love mirrors. I don't think you can ever have too many mirrors. If you are starting out, you can find great mirrors for a lot less than you can find a painting. You can put more than one mirror in a room. I've had mirrors made out of old doorframes. I found these pine doorframes, and they were so cheap that I just had them made into mirrors. I think they help make a small room look bigger. They reflect light. They help a dark room because they bounce light around. You can put them over something and you put lamps in front of them. I would fill up a room with mirrors until I could start to buy pictures. I think that is always the dilemma of art—it ends up being expensive.

LIBBY CAMERON You don't come in to your living room and typically stand; you are hopefully sitting if the room is working right, so it's important to see things closer to eye level. I love discovering pictures that I didn't notice when I first walked into a room.

BRIAN McCARTHY I know a lot of people who are fearful of hanging art themselves. One person holds it and just moves it up and down a little, and you look at it in relation to what's sitting above or behind and also where it's hanging relative to other art in the room. For instance, in this room the wall with the fireplace becomes the first wall you are going to hang a picture on, as it is what you see when you walk in, and then things are going to begin to take on a relationship to that as you move around the room. So you want to start at that point because that is going to give you the basis from which everything else is hung.

SUZANNE TUCKER USED A BLACK-AND-WHITE WALLPAPER TO ACCENT THE MIRROR IN A SMALL BATHROOM, ADDING A WHIMSICAL AND LIVELY FEEL TO A VERY SMALL SPACE.

THIS MIRROR REFLECTS A COUPLE'S LIVING ROOM; IT WAS HER WEDDING PRESENT TO HIM.

Mita Corsini Bland

BUNNY WILLIAMS'S KIPS BAY SHOW HOUSE ROOM OFFERS AN INTERESTING
COMBINATION OF PAINTED WALL PANELS AND A MIRROR HUNG ON A MIRROR,
ADDING MORE LIGHT AND DEPTH.

LIGHTING

I personally try to avoid all ceiling lights because I think that overhead light is a tragedy, and I think there is no point. ALBERT HADLEY

LIBBY CAMERON I had a lovely friend who died several years ago. Sally lived on the East River and had the most incredible art collection. She and her husband started collecting modern art in the twenties. They had six big Picassos upstairs in their library beyond the bedroom; *Women of Algiers* was the biggest of the canvases, and they had three small lamps in the room—that was it. Downstairs they had huge Frank Stellas and some very large works by Jasper Johns, oils from his gray period. There were a couple of cans in the dining room ceiling and a lantern in the front hall, but that was it. It always amazed me that the lack of lighting had no effect on what you saw. Those paintings were so powerful on their own that they almost didn't need to be lit.

I find that many houses have ceilings that look like Swiss cheese—just filled with holes. Luckily, recessed lights today are more subtle than the ones from years ago, which were the size of dinner plates. Today, there is a wider variety of lighting options. In my office, we have halogen lights, which throw off a lot of heat, which is a good thing as I rarely turn my heat up above sixty in the winter. I like romantic lighting, ambient lighting, as opposed to harsh overhead lighting. I like lighting that feels like a campfire, creating a glow. Clients with amazing art collections have different requirements certainly. It has all become very high tech—I can't figure out how to even use some of the switches today—they are computerized. I like to walk into a room and flick the simple toggle switch and bingo, have light from a few lamps or from a lantern or fixture overhead.

EMMA BURNS Floor plans are totally important because then you can establish your lighting—find out whether your lighting points are in the right places or whether you need to redo that, how many sockets you are going to have in the room so you can control the lighting. I don't like much overhead lighting. I don't like very sophisticated lighting schemes at all—in fact, they scare me. I like table lamps, which are pretty basic these days, but I think work the best. I don't want to have a hideous little laminated card by the switch plate explaining to me what it is because it's so sophisticated that nobody understands it—only the person who designs it. I particularly fall back on the dimmer switch and maybe candles even.

ALBERT HADLEY There are so many ways that one can subtly light a room to get light that is both flattering and functional. Some form of shaded light and lamplight is important. It doesn't all have to be traditional forms or materials, but I like light that is filtered and has a certain ambience. There are a lot of good fixtures to light artwork that give a glow to a space. We do want to eliminate as many dark creepy corners as possible, but I don't think that a room that is overly illuminated is an agreeable space.

If you are using a pair of lamps they should be on the same level because they make an architectural statement. But I don't think just because you have tall lamps you can't have a little one here and there. There is nothing more disturbing than having pairs of things that are not paired—it's like a lame duck. I think too often lamps get so high over your head that you are sitting under the light. So many people put standing lamps with the shades up high and then you look up and see nothing but the bulb and a glaring light.

PETER DUNHAM I think lighting can either make or break or room. It's either gloomy or it's warm—there is a very fine line. I always want to go to warm lighting. Even in very contemporary places, I try to use lighting that comes from a lot of different sources, whether it's lighting on the art, on the bookcases, or behind a tree, or lamps. You try to mix it up. I get very nervous when people say I want a lot of light—they start terrifying me—they want fifty-five cans in the ceiling. I don't like glaring lights. As I said, there is a fine line; you don't want it to feel gloomy and depressed. I like tons of lamps and reading lights everywhere.

DANIEL ROMUALDEZ I really try my best to talk clients out of high hats in their apartments or houses. We are going to such effort—and I just don't think they do justice to a room. But you can't win that battle every time. It's more work for us to find lamps and get the light in levels, but I just think there is nothing better than old-fashioned lamps. Lots of lamps—you have to just keep selling. And absolutely, it should be at different heights.

CATHY KINCAID Lighting needs to come from all different angles, and I am sure everyone has said that—that's just Decorating 101. You don't want a chandelier with all the bulbs exposed and no other light in the room. It's not going to be comfortable. You definitely need recessed lights that are architectural, that are innocuous. You need to light a coffee table, to light objects, to light a mantel or artwork. Supposedly if you light a table, the light bounces back up and makes the people sitting around that table glow. Lighting consultants are extremely important. They know exactly which lights to use and how to place them. You have to let the consultant know where you are using mirrors and where you are putting artwork. Then you go and you start layering, with your chandelier or a lantern, and you put sconces over the fireplace or on bookshelves—we do a lot of lighting on bookshelves. Then you go to your next level and you put your lamps on your tables. I think it's important to mix a lot of different types of lamps and not have too many. You want to make sure you have opaque shades in some places and shades you can see through when you need it for reading.

THE GLASS LAMP WITH ITS SIMPLE PLEATED SHADE BRINGS AN INTIMATE LIGHT TO A LARGE PANELED LIBRARY.

BUNNY WILLIAMS The interesting thing is, I find the older I get the more light I need. I go in my apartment and I think the bulbs are out and it's just me. I think that whenever I am working on a new job. I do get lighting in the ceiling but not just with high hats. We try interesting ways of getting some ceiling light, even for people who have a really traditional house. Some of those beautiful surface-mounted lights—they are Italian, very modern, and the light heads are small—can just light the wall. Good light in a room needs to come from several sources—from overhead and eye level.

JEFFREY BILHUBER Chandeliers I love, where basically the entire room can be lit up. I love lamps. I can sit in a dark room with one lamp on for weeks and not be depressed. Understanding the infiltration of natural daylight is also really important. I don't think it's critical because you can falsify that. Many times you will hear potential clients say, "Well, I think the next step is for you to come to the house and see how the light moves through the room during the day." I say, "I get it. I can figure that part out. Last time I looked the sun rises in the east and it sets in the west, and I understand." If it's north-facing you get even filtered light all day long. We get that part.

It's a lot of silliness someone saying I have to live in my house before I engage in decorating. A great decorator should be able to understand instantaneously how it will work and what should work better.

BRIAN McCARTHY Thinking about recessed lighting now, you have all these options for square aperture versus round. In the old days, what were your options with recessed light? The fixtures looked like dinner plates. So you had these huge cutouts. That's not your only option now, so you can do things that are quite small and discreet.

EMMA BURNS I like soft picture lighting. I am passionate about paintings and I do love them to be lit, but I don't love that lighting on the painting where you get a cold, clear light—like a gallery light. I like paintings to be a focal point, but at the same time part of the background of the room, not really a "look at me" piece. I love the shades to be lined in gold; it pulls the light down and you get lovely pools of light.

PAUL VINCENT WISEMAN Ideally, each table would have a glow and we would sense the light coming from those sconces and we wouldn't quite understand where the light was coming from. I make it look like it's all coming from the lamps. It's very, very complex, but that's what lighting is about. Candlelight is still extremely important. All you have to do is light one candle and people respond.

SUZANNE RHEINSTEIN The husband of one of my friends said, "I am really glad I'm not in charge of the candle bills in this house." Is there anything better? Is there anything better than a log fire to greet you? My husband says he going to spend his last five dollars on firewood.

A PORCELAIN PHEASANT TURNED INTO A LAMP ADDS INTEREST AS WELL AS A SOURCE OF LIGHT.

PAUL VINCENT WISEMAN There was something in the *New York Times* the other day about that. The creative process cannot be translated onto a computer. Ideas are visual. When I draw a lampshade it's a proportion, a relationship, and that you can't do on a computer.

BRIAN McCARTHY Again there has to be a point of view as to how you are going to finish your lamps. I think you can have a little variety. To me it's all about layers—I love the layers. Lampshades can incorporate color successfully where a lot of people just want to have off- white lampshades. There are different shades of golds, and instead of just lining it in white, it could be lined in a shell pink. Things like that help with the quality of light in a room.

WILLIAM HODGINS Madam was very careful about lighting. Wherever you were, you were supposed to be able to read. Not that I ever saw her read anything, ever.

SUSAN BARTLETT CRATER My grandparents used candles a lot at night, particularly in New York. Sister loved long black candles in gold candlesticks in the dining room. You always felt there was this shimmery soft light everywhere when you walked into the apartment at night. There was the light from the lit fire, multiple candles everywhere, and what lamps were lit always seemed to throw off a soft and gentle light. Her lampshades were frequently lined with pink silk, and she liked to use pretty fabrics on the shades with some kind of simple trim. She used paper shades in Maine with decoupage that was outlined by tiny pinpricked holes, which the light would come through. She made these herself and they provided a soft, diffused light that gave a welcoming feeling to her houses.

She frequently had a Rigaud candle lit in the sitting room and of course fresh flowers everywhere. At Christmas her apartment always smelled like paperwhites and dark green Rigaud candles. Her lighting set the mood for a glamorous evening where people, who were definitely more important than the setting, were put in the mood to have fun.

FURNITURE

THIS DRAWING ROOM BY BUNNY WILLIAMS FEATURES A VARIETY OF DIFFERENT
FURNITURE STYLES. THERE IS A WONDERFUL SENSE OF SCALE IN THIS ROOM.

My great-uncle Rory Cameron was known as "the man with perfect taste," a phrase coined by a British journalist. He had an unerring sense of taste, though he was always embarrassed by this reputation, of being famous for living well. He said, "It's enough to live comfortably, to keep things in scale and be content with your lot." The house Rory is most renowned for is La Fiorentina, which has been written about by many. Part of its allure was Rory's mother, Enid, the Countess of Kenmare, a great Australian beauty who conquered many hearts. The house was encircled by the Mediterranean on the tip of Saint-Jean-Cap-Ferrat, overlooking Beaulieu Bay. During the war, the Germans took over La Fiorentina, built fortifications, and then blew them up, virtually destroying the Florentine house that had existed by the time they left. Rory rebuilt La Fiorentina after the war; the house was a shell and in shambles. He used to laugh when describing it, and said that actually its condition saved him a lot of work. Rory's inspiration for the façade came from Palladio's Villa Rotunda. He made the rooms smaller, added larger windows, and used colors that were muted and matte—umbers, buffs, lemon yellows, eggshell blues, and every gradation of white you could imagine. He painted the walls of the eight-windowed living room the color of the backside of an olive leaf, which he always said was his favorite color, and filled the house with uncompromisingly good furniture, a good portion of it museum quality, mixed in with a few Jean Michel Frank pieces as well as priceless objects and paintings.

Rory appreciated and had beautiful furniture: Hepplewhite chests, Louis XVI chairs, eighteenth-century Ming tables, and Queen Anne needlepoint rugs. He had the Regency gong that George IV used at Brighton Pavilion to summon his guests to dinner, a wonderful pair of William Morris sunflower-shaped andirons that were made for his grandfather—my great-great-grandfather— and wooden lions once used to support the bed of the last dowager Empress of China as the surround for a coffee table. He had wonderful art and paintings, Giambologna bronzes, Rodin statues, Song dynasty horses, Ingres drawings, and paintings that ran the gamut from Uccello to Oudry to Stubbs and

RORY CAMERON'S
INSPIRATION FOR
THE FAÇADE FOR LA
FIORENTINA CAME
FROM PALLADIO'S VILLA
ROTUNDA.

Landseer. Rory liked large, calm pieces of furniture and never wanted furniture to dominate a room. He had an infallible sense of how to mix and mate furniture—that was his genius. He was very tactile and had a fingertip feel for things; touch and texture were essential to him. I can't remember a time when sitting with him that he wouldn't hold on to my hand and spin the rings on my finger around and around while talking. Rory always touched the walls and fabrics on upholstery and would go through a room feeling the objects, opening and closing the lids on boxes.

Les Quatres Sources is the name of the house that Rory rebuilt when he moved to Provence to escape the masses of people on the Riviera. It was on a slope of land just behind a raisin field and was comprised of two stark, geometric buildings on several levels. The house was built out of the regional stone, much of it from the original seventeenth-century farmhouse that had stood on the land. Inside, it was muted and soft, merely a backdrop for a variety and mixture of beautiful furniture. The backgrounds were light and airy, and very textural, with stone floors and chalky plaster walls, sisal rugs and baskets juxtaposed with amazing furniture. There was a Duncan Phyfe settee under a portrait of my great-grandmother and her two sisters, covered in a simple, nubbly Indian cotton weave. There was a wonderful bronze Italian statue of Neptune at the top and beginning of the stone staircase that went from the entrance hall down to the corridor that led to the living room. The staircase was beautiful and sculptural; it looked like the inside curl of a conch shell. Rory had a wonderful appreciation for opulence combined with understatement. He was able to edit out the boredom in furniture, of too many tables and chairs, of too much wood, and was able to combine the unexpected—the old and the new. Despite the grandeur with which he grew up, Rory was very low-key, unassuming and gentle, and such fun to be with. He certainly had a fascinating life. He was the third person to enter King Tutankhamen's tomb in Egypt with his mother and Howard Carter, and told me about the footsteps he saw that were still in the sand floor. He loved to travel and wrote several history and travel books about India and Australia—places that he loved and visited often. He was a fabulous raconteur and had a beguiling way of telling stories. Years ago I had lunch with Rory and Kenny Lane at an Indian restaurant above the Paris movie theater next to the Plaza Hotel. The restaurant was very atmospheric and we sat on mats at a low table. I remember feeling transported and mesmerized listening to Rory's stories about India—he had that wonderful ability of piquing your imagination.

Rory loved his dogs almost more than people. When I was little he had both whippets and pugs, but he had mixed breeds when he moved to Ménerbes, his house in Provence. It wasn't uncommon for a dogfight to break out under the lunch or dinner table. Rory was never fazed by these brawls and would simply say in a slightly louder than normal voice, "Shoo, shoo. Go away."

When with Rory, Lady Diana Cooper said she knew "the elegance and the comfort and the glorious pleasure of being with someone who really knows how to do things. One meets only three or four such people in a lifetime, and I am not sure that there are any others left."

—LIBBY CAMERON

THE SOFA AND SOFA TABLE IN THE MIDDLE OF THE LIVING ROOM ANCHOR THE
ROOM IN THIS LARGE UPPER WEST SIDE APARTMENT IN NEW YORK CITY.

ANCHORING a ROOM

A living room should have a couple of good pieces of furniture, even if it is just a great coffee table or a very simple end table—everything else can be decoration. A good coffee table and a good mirror and upholstered furniture can usually anchor any room, don't you agree? JOHN ROSSELLI

LIBBY CAMERON At Parish-Hadley, one of the first things we did when starting a job was to suggest different upholstery models to clients. Oftentimes, clients wanted to go to the upholstery shops and actually sit in the chairs, which is a good thing, as they all do really feel very different. There are a lot of options and details to consider—the height and depth of the arms, loose seats, tight seats, tufted seats, loose backs, tight backs, the shape and pitch of the chair, the seat height, seat depth. There are also many things to take into account—the size, the length, the overall height given the ceiling height of the room, but most important, the size of the piece in relation to the other pieces in the room. Taking clients to sit on furniture is important if they have the interest; I always think of Goldilocks—one is too big, one is too small, and then they find one that is just right.

Mrs. Parish and Albert liked certain models. Mrs. Parish liked the Carr sofa, which had big soft, rounded arms; Albert prefers more tailored models, like the St. Thomas sofa, or models that are more stylized, never clunky. He had a wonderful sofa in his house in Southport, which was quite low and fit just perfectly in the far corner of his living room. It had a flat border along the edge of the low, tufted back and a plain, tight seat. It was small and was detailed beautifully. Albert always details pieces in a very customized way, which is wonderful to be able to do.

DANIEL ROMUALDEZ I think this is important: if a client isn't really into collecting antiques, I try and talk them into having some sculptural antiques that function as something—it could be their telephone table. In traditional decorating every piece is beautiful and has a shape. So in a modern instance, I try to get them to do something interesting. If they won't go for something antique, I try to introduce at least something—it might be midcentury—that has some patina and a great shape. I think it is too dull if everything is upholstered.

TODD ROMANO Some clients will become fixated on one object and they will lose track of the fact that everything is connected to something else. None of these things float independently—or very rarely do they. I mean they might have some incredible Picasso and that might be the only thing on that wall, but even that doesn't really function independently because it is going to need to have a connection going around the room. People will get fixated on one thing and not see that bigger picture. I love playing with scale. I have a funny little collection of antique small chairs. I love big things, I love small things, and I love to balance those out. One of my favorite things when we are actually installing a room—when we arrive with all the accessories and the different art objects—is arranging it all. I love using trays on top of tables or little stands, even if you are just putting a pot with an orchid on it.

CARLETON VARNEY Dorothy Draper's sense of balance was never the equation of match and match. It was always weight versus weight, and what I learned from her is that no matter what you put on the plan—you can draw pretty plans with sofas and put the chair here and this there and show it to the client—it means absolutely nothing. The decorators and designers of today fail to realize that furniture has bulk and to envision what it looks like in the bulk stage as opposed to the line stage. So, Dorothy, being a very big woman (she was six foot one), liked things big and comfortable. She didn't like anything ditzy. The only thing that Dorothy liked that was ditzy was Hope Hampton, who was her friend. Hope used to come in to the office with that blond hair—she was a showgirl and the two of them were so in contrast to one another. You would see this tall woman and then you would see Hope. Dorothy always wanted to have Hope's nose. Hope had this little nose and Dorothy had this wonderful patrician nose.

THE SOFA

I think you have to start with one thing—like where the sofa is going. That anchors a room, a major piece, something big—something that looks gutsy.

MARIO BUATTA

LIBBY CAMERON The sofa is most often the anchor in a room. Too many chairs, alike or different, will make a room feel fractured and like a furniture showroom. People tend to sit in clusters, or they want to lie down and stretch out or curl their feet up under them, but not always sit in straight-backed wooden armchairs. A sofa is one of the most important pieces of furniture in a room. You should feel drawn to it, you should want to sit on it or snooze on it. It's a big element and dictates how the room is laid out and how it works.

TODD ROMANO Absolutely. My parents have a sofa that was made for my grandparents' house in 1938. It's a Charles of London sofa. When I was a little boy, it was in our living room, then it went into my parents' sitting room and became Daddy's nap sofa. I got it when we redid the back house for me—that became my little pad. We called it the "Taj Garage." Then it went with me to Colorado Springs, where I lived for a year before I moved here. Next it went back to Texas and was reupholstered, and is in my parents' big great room in the country. That sofa is seventy years old. Good things like that will last forever. Good upholstery is good upholstery. So yes, I always encourage people—I would rather them buy less but better, and something they truly love. Especially when it comes to antiques and art, you want to buy things that you really love. Don't worry about the value of it.

THE ST. THOMAS SOFA IS A POPULAR CUSTOM-MADE MODEL.

EMMA BURNS Once I have established the shape of the room and once I know how it is going

THIS MODEL IS A
VARIATION OF A CHAIR
NAMED AND MADE FOR
WILLIAM PALEY.

to operate, then the furniture becomes important. I figure out the length of a three-piece sofa or if it is an L-shape, and if it has a skirt or a fringe, and what sort of legs to have. I think about which other chairs in the room have legs and what's the balance—so that we don't have a room full of only legs or skirts.

WILLIAM HODGINS I always tell people to get the best sofa you possibly can—the same for all the upholstered things. I think that's very serious for young people to buy good furniture because it goes from house to house. Well, it does seem sort of foolish to spend $12,000 for a sofa when you can buy one for $2,000, but Mrs. Parish would never have bothered saying that—it just wasn't part of her vocabulary. "Just get the right one, that's it."

LIBBY CAMERON More and more, people buy upholstery from catalogues: Pottery Barn, Williams-Sonoma Home, or Crate & Barrel. They see pieces on the floor in those huge spaces, but they can't make the translation in their mind of the proportion and how it will fit into their apartment or house. Those pieces of upholstery are all based on the great models that come from the wonderful upholstery shops, where the great furniture is still made that will last for years and years. They are not bad, at all, but they aren't very well made or as comfortable. Something about these catalogue pieces is off; I think it is the lack of detail, the softness of the cushions, the pitch of the back or of the seat, and the proportion is just not quite right. If possible, I think people should splurge and buy a really good custom-made sofa; it will last for years and years, and a classic well-proportioned design will always work almost anywhere with anything—new or old.

BRIAN McCARTHY Something else people need to keep in mind is the shape and style of upholstery and how that plays into a room because it really can impact a room tremendously, since it becomes the silhouette or profile you are looking at. So when you are thinking of the upholstery, are you walking in and looking at it from the side? Are you looking at it straight on? Are you looking at it from a three-quarter view or are you walking in behind it? What does the back of it look like? You might want to think about the back of the sofa having a little bit of shape or the back of the chair having a scroll.

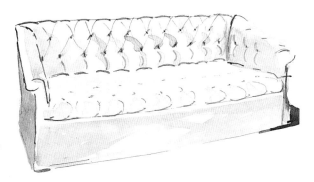

MILES REDD A layman might do two sofas, as some people do, which is always to me an uninteresting room arrangement. It looks hotel-ish. I think the curiosity of decoration is objects, and chairs are probably the most unusual objects, so I always tend to have groupings of chairs rather than multiple sofas, because even though you may have three on a sofa, no one ever really does.

NAMED FOR THE WHITNEYS, THIS MODEL WAS USED IN MANY OF THEIR HOUSES; IT IS A VARIATION OF A CLASSIC TUXEDO SOFA.

BUNNY WILLIAMS Nobody sits in the middle of a sofa. That's why I say a sofa never really needs to be much longer than 7 feet, unless you entertain a lot and are going to do a big banquette that's very long. But in the average house, a sofa never really needs to be longer than 7 feet. A sofa that goes into a corner can work—it depends on the room. I have made sectionals and people just love them; it was just what the room called for—for watching television and lounging. You can pile a lot of people on it and kids love it, and somebody can sit comfortably in the middle. So it can work, but it doesn't work in a living room which is more for conversation.

SCALE

There has to be a continuity of taste. The educated eye selects within a frame-work; textiles, furniture, and paintings will then form a whole. In my apart-ment, for example, a 1930s end table is paired with a Louis XVI chair. What they have in common is an aesthetic honesty of form. ALBERT HADLEY

LIBBY CAMERON Albert and I worked on a house together years ago for a couple who had bought a big house on a lovely piece of land. Their old house was much smaller, so we really had to start from scratch. They had a few pieces that worked but the scale of the new house was so different from the old one that their furniture looked dwarfed in the new vast rooms. Their rugs were all too small, so I had to find new rugs.

Typically when beginning a job at Parish-Hadley, we would work off of a floor plan and know what worked, what existed, and where the holes were. There wasn't always a set rule about the rug or the color and fabric scheme of a room, and which came first. In this instance, I seem to remember working from the fabrics to find a rug. These clients were in the office one day and I had had four or five rugs brought over for them to look at. I thought one was just perfect and Albert concurred. We showed that one first and told them we thought it was just right. Well, then the question of its age and value came up. It was an antique rug but was also in beautiful condition. She loved it but he was just quiet and looked a little bit stormy. The meeting went on; I could feel his distraction. We left it that I would meet with them the following day in the country with the rug, and that we would decide whether or not it was the one once it was in the room. The rug went down, the furniture went on it. I would have kept it if it were for my house. He walked in and said, "I don't want that old moth-eaten thing. Find me a new rug." Each to his own. I did find another rug, but it didn't have the same depth or warmth that the old one did.

THE VARIETY AND DIFFERENCES IN THE SCALE OF THE FURNITURE ADD CHARM TO THIS BEDROOM.

SUSAN BARTLETT CRATER My grandmother said every room should have a "personality" chair. Many times they were totally out of proportion to the room, but that was what gave them interest and an element of surprise. She loved miniature upholstered children's chairs and sofas and would use them often. In the first house she decorated in Far Hills, the one where she experimented with painted floors and furniture, curtains made out of mattress ticking, and other innovations, she had these tiny Victorian chairs that were upholstered in red satin. My mother and Aunt D.B. loved to sit in them when they were about five and six, and they fit in them just perfectly. They were in front of the fireplace. They are like tiny beautiful Stuart Little furniture and children still clamor to sit in them today. My mother has them in front of the fireplace in her apartment in Boston. Sister's close friend, the wonderful artist Mari Watts Hitchcock, was a frequent visitor to the house in Far Hills and described the living room to me. "It was a dream. Sister always had everything different from anyone else. Sister had these really teeny love seats on each side of the fireplace. People laughed at that, but it was very much like doing a painting: if you love something then you put it in." It's that wonderful element of surprise with those beautiful little chairs that makes the room so great.

A HORSEGUARD SOFA HAS HAD TUFTING ADDED TO THE BACK TO ALTER ITS APPEARANCE.

LIBBY CAMERON I've had Aiken sofas made for clients and they are the most wonderful, comfortable sofas. They originated in Aiken, South Carolina, and are painted wooden frames that have, quite literally, a mattress as the seat cushion in one piece, and there are three back pillows, a pillow at each end, and then there are usually masses of throw pillows to boot. They do have that Southern feel and appeal, of leisure and pleasure. There is no better place to take

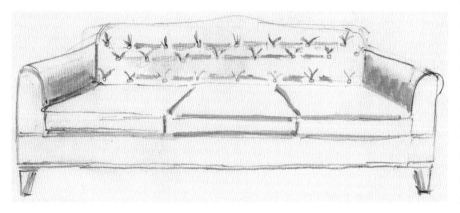

a nap than on one of those sofas. Mrs. Parish loved them and many of our clients had them on their porches or in their houses.

PETER DUNHAM You need that, something quirky that you had growing up or that you found on the side of the street. I like the idea of there being memories. Houses are really a reflection of the people in them.

ALBERT HADLEY When you think of Sis's houses in Maine and even her apartment in the city, there were mixtures of things, but it was all very subtle because they all were the same aesthetic. They weren't necessarily from the same period or the same country, but they all felt right together. You can buy a perfectly beautiful French Louis XVI armchair and have it upholstered. If it is for a room that has no other French furniture in it, it will look like it has come from a thrift shop. It's that kind of thing that you can't do. If you bring in one French chair, it's got to have some company, otherwise there is no point.

EMMA BURNS I like painted furniture. I quite like fruitwood. I like quirky furniture. I like more and more the more I learn. I love beautiful English Country furniture without a doubt. But I love twentieth-century furniture now and pieces from the 1930s and '40s. My eye has adjusted over the years. I don't like aggressive pieces. I like a little bit of a twist and a bit of humor about it. It's that thing of just slightly putting things off balance. So it's not all predicted.

LIBBY CAMERON I spent a lot of time shopping for furniture and antiques with Mrs. Parish. She would go into shops and poke around. She was always very friendly and nice to all the vendors, but she wasn't as interested in chitchat. We would go to fifteen or twenty shops in a day so there wasn't time for conversation; she was on a mission. It was exhausting keeping up with her, trying to be where she was because it was all in her head—what would go where. She chose pieces, which 95 percent of the time would work and end up with the clients. I would have a list of what was still needed—the pair of something for a mantel, a table or bench, or interesting brackets because the client had a pair of something to put on them. Most often, Mrs. Parish would say to go find things that I liked and found interesting, and to get pictures to show her.

BUNNY WILLIAMS I think that the reason I like to mix it up is because then you really see the individual things. If you have painted chairs around a wood table, they become more interesting; you see the painted chairs and you see the wood table. If you have a mahogany table and mahogany chairs, they all meld into each other. Even all white melds together. Again I like mixing periods because if I have something that is complicated, I like to put it next to something that is simple. I think the juxtaposition makes them more interesting. I may find a wonderful little Victorian chair that I love, but then I might put it next to a square slipper chair—just something that makes it interesting because it then becomes a thing on its own. I think that is the hardest thing to do—to know how to combine and mix. That is real personal taste. It is something that when it is well done, it works, but it is hard to teach it and it is hard to get. You will know in a heartbeat that this chair is going to look great for this desk. If I had to explain it, I could tell you the reason why I have this Italian desk and I put this modern chair next to it, because the desk is painted wood and I decided I wanted a metal chair. I could give you all the reasons, but you just see it. In a funny way you don't want to make rules, you just want comfort and warmth and accessibility.

MARIO BUATTA I had a chair that I bought at a thrift shop and had slipcovered very loosely. Albert walked in and asked who made that cover? I had had the man cut it and make it very loose, and the man questioned me, "Are you sure?" and I said yes. Then Albert said, "It's fabulous," and he took it, turned and adjusted it. I learned more that evening when Albert came for a drink than I would have learned at school for four years. Just moving it made the whole thing look different—he has a wonderful spatial sense and he is a very good teacher. Some of his students still carry it—you have it—I see it in your work, Libby. You have Albert's sense of placement. Some rooms you see these days have fourteen different chairs in them. Isn't it amazing? They have a Louis and Hooey and Sammy and Harry—what are people thinking or doing?

Dear Sister,
    Thank you so much for letting me spend a lovely afternoon sketching with you. When Random House is through with it, I'll send the real thing to you.
    Merry Christmas to you all.

    Love,
    Duane & Mark

ONE OF SEVERAL SEATING AREAS IN SISTER PARISH'S FIFTH AVENUE LIVING
ROOM CENTERS ON THE BEAUTIFULLY DETAILED VICTORIAN SOFA, AN
ASSORTMENT OF PAINTED TABLES, AND THE ELABORATE CURTAINS. THE
COMBINATION CREATES AN INTIMATE AREA IN A LARGE DRAWING ROOM. THIS
WATERCOLOR IS BY MARK HAMPTON.

ECLECTIC MIXES

I can't tell you how many people say, "Well, this was Aunt Edna's Victorian parlor set and I have to use it." The next question I will ask is, "Do you like it?" and when they say no, then I tell them not to use it—life is too short.

TODD ROMANO

TODD ROMANO Your Aunt Edna loved this, but you don't. There are many different ways that you can honor your Aunt Edna and not be tortured by having to stare at her Victorian parlor set. If it is something that they did on their own, then I try to be respectful of that and find a way to fit it in, even if I don't like it. I have had to do that on many occasions. I think we all do. Even with the best of clients and the best of jobs and the best of budgets and architecture, there is always an element of compromise involved in our business. How do you deal with a collection of objects that perhaps doesn't ring your bell, but the client loves them.

PAUL VINCENT WISEMAN Can you imagine walking into a client's house that had a jukebox, a Wurlitzer—a good one? I had clients that had Andy Warhols and a very eclectic mix of things—the jukebox, this wild antique fabric collection—and they bought this amazing house, so I said, "What are we going to do with this?" So we organized the antique fabrics. I even had a museum person take the antique fabrics and turn them into pillows without destroying them. I found a sideboard, a Scottish nineteenth-century altar table from a church for their dining room, and brought it all together—the Knoll chairs and the Warhols. This was twenty years ago. If I really hate what the clients have, I work around it and slowly keep moving it upstairs or down to the basement, until they understand why it doesn't have a relationship. It's all about relationships. I say it's not that this piece is ugly—this piece doesn't have any relationship to what you are trying to do. Grandma's rocking chair from Maine doesn't work in your beach house in Malibu unless you're going to treat it like

sculpture and it's the only thing in front of your big picture window. Then it's fine. But if you think you're going to put it in with the other stuff, it's just not going to work. The intellectual thing—the big "I" word—it's okay; get people to intellectualize it, get them to see dimensionally, what's actually happening. We're not just making a pretty room. A reflection is dimensional. I think 3D all the time. I see in the dark. What does it look like in the dark? What do you look like in the dark? What are you thinking in the dark? I learn things that I don't really want to know.

CATHY KINCAID A lot of people will hate a chair that they have been looking at forever. They just didn't like it where it was, and then they realize that they love it in the new spot because it's more functional. I think it's very important that you don't just walk in and tell someone to get rid of everything. It's their home.

BUNNY WILLIAMS Do you know what's interesting? I tend to downplay heirlooms in the beginning, but I think what happens is that when you start showing people better things, they begin to realize what they have isn't so great. If it's something I really hate I say, "This can't go in the living room. You can put it in the guest bedroom if you have to have it because you can't give Granny's chest away." What I have found, and this is interesting, is that during the course of working with a client, as they begin to see better things and like them, they go back and look at that piece and realize that it's really ugly.

A LARGE-SCALE ENGLISH CHAIR FILLS A CORNER. IT IS WONDERFULLY DETAILED WITH BUTTONS AND NAILHEAD TRIM.

ALBERT HADLEY I had a letter from a woman the other day who sent along a picture she had of a pair of chairs. She went through the whole thing, describing them, that they are Henry XV, and she goes on with the description about the cabriole legs and the color of the wood—the whole thing. She wanted to know where she could send these chairs, and I said to Nancy, "Please write her back and give her the name of a shop that I think she should send them to, and that she can't use my name and Henry at the same time." That's just it, people don't know. Have you ever heard of Henry XV?

PETER DUNHAM I think a lot of people skimp on quality and they end up with things they get tired of very quickly. The things that I have spent the most on I treasure the most in a weird way. It doesn't mean that everything should be expensive, but there are certain things that I know I spent crazy amounts of money for. In my office I have this great red desk that I bought—I shudder at what I paid for it—I paid 10,000 pounds for it. This chipped red-painted desk from a Christopher Gibbs sale when he was selling off his country house. I love the desk and I cannot believe I paid that much money, but every time I walk into my office I think, "God, that's fabulous." I have had it ten years and every time I look at it I think, "Wow," whereas so many other things may have come and gone that I couldn't have cared less about. We have to educate people that there are certain things in the room that you've got to buy, one great piece of furniture or one amazing pair of consoles for the front hall that every time you come home and put the key in the door you're thinking, "Look, those are beautiful, I'm so glad I own them."

CATHY KINCAID Some people don't like antiques, especially people in Texas and people who were brought up without any money. We use a lot of reproduction chairs around dining room tables, because the antique furniture is just too fragile for most people to survive on. I have all mine being fixed. I love lacquer coffee tables and any type of cleaner piece of furniture to mix in with more traditional antiques. A contemporary piece of lacquered furniture or a Japanese table or Rosewood Japanese table is such a relief when you have Regency chairs and painted cabinets. I like to have a little bit of painted furniture in a room, but not all painted.

MARIO BUATTA I don't like really fancy stuff. Did you ever see Gregory Smith's bed? It has a headboard and footboard the same height and carved pagodas—it's brown chinoiserie. Supposedly it was made for Prince Albert to sleep in when he would go down to the Brighton Pavilion, which he never stayed at apparently. Derek Stevenson bought it and sold it to Gregory Smith, and Mrs. Davenport bought it from Gregory. It's in the McMillen book all over the place. So when Gregory was getting older, and I knew him, he said, "You have always loved that bed—I would like you to have it." He said for $2,500, so I bought it and I have been sleeping in it since 1976. So Sister called me one day and said, "Do you still have that bed—Gregory Smith's bed?" I can usually do her voice, I said, "Yes I do." She said, "I have a client who wants it." I said, "I am afraid it comes with a curse," and she said, "What's that?" I said, "Me, your client gets me and the bed." She said, "If things ever go bad, call me and I can sell it for you." I said, "Oh boy."

LIBBY CAMERON I loved reading about Eli Manning, the New York Giants' football player, last year before the Super Bowl and learning that he enjoyed spending afternoons antiquing with his mother as a child. It's great fun to go antiquing with someone and hear their impressions and to see what appeals to them. There is so much to learn about furniture—it wasn't all made to just look at. Some pieces are ingenious as well as functional, and have hidden drawers and multiple uses. You can learn so much about the culture of a period in history by studying furniture. My children are not very interested in going to antiques shops or shows with me. I love the idea of a football player being so interested in antiques—it's so great, don't you think?

TODD ROMANO I got dragged around with my parents. I would go to look at houses with them. I would go to antiques shops with them. I was very lucky to have a lot of their attention, and I got to spend a lot of time with them and absorb their interests inside and out—that's why I am sitting here today.

DANIEL ROMUALDEZ I remember Billy Baldwin saying it is really great to see a beautiful seventeenth-century Japanese lacquered table and have nothing but a basket on top of it. If everything is too beautiful and grand, they cancel each other out, and if everything is too modern, they cancel each other out. So I am a great believer of the high and low mix; of things often not being so perfect and pretty, and that being mixed in with something really beautiful is fun, and it all comes together.

JOHN ROSSELLI Anything that is good is good. I think you can certainly put a classical French piece of furniture in a contemporary room and in a minimalist room. Decoration has changed in the sense that everything is so expensive. The most amusing and beautiful things are so difficult to find, hence the surge of reproductions.

KATHRYN IRELAND What is America's obsession with reproductions? Maybe it's not on the East Coast but on the West Coast, every decorator uses reproductions—their jobs are so easy—whereas I scour the planet looking for unusual, different pieces. I realize that all the other decorators in Southern California go to Blue Whale and order the chinoiserie cupboard. It's horrifying to me, the bad taste. They all think that it's marvelous. They have no point of reference—their point of reference is the designers that say, "Would you like to buy reproductions?" It's much easier to just go and order the table: they don't have to deal with the shipping, they don't have to go to London or Paris, and

AN ENGLISH PEMBROKE TABLE WHEN OPENED PROVIDES A SURFACE FOR OBJECTS; THE SMALL MODERN TABLE BENEATH IT ADDS AN INTERESTING CONTRAST OF COLOR AND TEXTURE.

they don't have to deal with the refinisher. For me, it's all about the chase and the find.

MARTHA ANGUS You have to explain to them this isn't Seventh Avenue, you need to have some longevity built into your furniture. I actually feel like you should be able to buy furniture and have it forever. Maybe you switch out things, like throws and pillows, and the carpet that wears out, but not the furniture.

MARIO BUATTA I used to love to play tricks on Mrs. Parish. One time I went to see Margaret Parker—do you remember Margaret, on Chapel Street right behind Harrods? She used to work at Colefax. She was an unmarried woman and she wore a Hermès scarf around her head all the time. She always had on a lot of makeup, big lips. She had a very squeaky voice. So I go in one day and she said they were about to get a shipment and that on the way home you have to stop in and see. I said, "I'll have clients with me, I can't." "Then stop by early in the morning." So I said, "I'll look in the window and leave you a note." So I left her a long sheet, "I'll take this, this and this and that," and signed, Sister Parish. So the next day she called the Parish-Hadley office. Shortly thereafter, Sister Parish called and said, "Is this one of your tricks, one of your jokes?" Well, that sure did backfire.

LIBBY CAMERON I think that there should be a timelessness to design. I wonder how all of the new pieces and the trends will hold up—the markets are flooded with new and old, good and bad versions of classic designs and shapes. Where does a person begin when starting to design a space? Magazines and books are certainly great sources of information, but there is another level to it all, an understanding and knowledge about scale and why what works works. People should really take the time to learn and to ask questions when buying something and to find out where it came from. People are in a rush and want to instantly fill their spaces and make an instant house. Taste and style mature and evolve; it's hard to hold onto that idea when there's such a candy land of choices so readily available.

SUZANNE RHEINSTEIN Magazines do show us beautiful rooms. Remember when the English room was the be-all and end-all? People wanted that look and filled their houses with copies—bad reproduction furniture. Why not search for the one-of-a-kind thing? It doesn't have to be old. There are good things that come out of catalogs, but it is pathetic and sad to see entire rooms filled with bad reproductions. The furniture is clunky and brown. I really don't believe that a copy has to be bad; it can have character.

JEFFREY BILHUBER As I get older and mature, my work does too. I am increasingly drawn to much more traditional forms and finishes. It's simply the by-product of reaching middle age—you have to. We go further back in order to understand and embrace historically what has worked before, and why it has worked and given us comfort. We also still have to feel as if we live in our time and of our time. None of my rooms—which are as traditional as I can make them if that's what I want—none of my rooms are nostalgic, nor do any of my clients yearn to be in any other time or any other place. No one comes to me because they want to live in eighteenth-century France. What's the point?

THIS CHAIR, AN OLD FAMILY HEIRLOOM, HAS WONDERFUL NAILHEAD DETAILING ON THE APRON OF THE SEAT.

ALBERT HADLEY When I first started with Sis, she and Ann Bronfman were buying only Louis furniture. All this French furniture was really like sculpture in the space of the apartment. In the entrance hall, there was a marvelous Louis XVI console, and next to it was a piece of modern sculpture.

The time came to put furniture in and the big sofa went on the long wall and there was a seating group next to it, and a piano opposite the sofa. It was sparsely furnished, but it was comfortable, and there was a wonderful big rug for the whole thing. The beautiful antique furniture they chose was absolutely right—it was sculpture in that very modern open apartment.

BUNNY WILLIAMS When you see really beautiful wood—you know. Eighteenth-century faded mahogany, that's worth preserving. But 1950s sprayed lacquer red mahogany is not worth saving.

SUSAN BARTLETT CRATER Some people have this reverence for all kinds of wood and never want to paint it. I love brown furniture as much as the next person, if it's good, but it's not my religion. I am not someone who worships the natural beauty of all wood just because it's wood, and I don't mind painting something that would look much better in an altered state. If the floor is wood and it's fake parquet or the chair is just plain ugly, why not? When *House and Garden* first published photographs of the dark wood dining room chairs Sister had painted white, the editors called it "a decorating shot heard round the world." Many people thought it was sacrilegious, even though artists have been painting wood furniture for centuries. I have suggested painting things people have inherited and they look at me like I've told them to burn down their house. My mother paints everything so I guess I am used to it. She says a coat of paint really can turn an ugly duckling into a swan.

WILLIAM HODGINS As Mrs. P. used to say, "brown furniture"—she could say "BROWN" like, "Oh my god." Like it was the worst thing in the world. I actually find it nice. It took me a long time to get over it.

LIBBY CAMERON I love the mix of wood types with painted and lacquer furniture more than only wood furniture in a room. I love lacquer furniture, whether it's red, green, black, or brown lacquer—I like the finish, and I like creamy white and gilt wood furniture. Mrs. Parish always urged me to mix it up and not use "a suite of brown" anywhere. I've always used a variety of shapes and woods and finishes of furniture and periods of furniture. The variety adds interest. If everything in a room is brown wood, don't you think it flattens a room?

WILLIAM HODGINS It's boring—boring as can be. With Madam, though, you had to have the eye to pick up that piece of throwaway furniture and paint it up—she loved to do that.

JOHN ROSSELLI I'll never forget Mrs. Parish saying, "Well, Parish-Hadley has no more than three pieces of brown furniture in a room." That was her formula. Everything had to be mixed and matched and that's the way it worked. She had a bedroom that had a painted bed, a mahogany chest of drawers, mahogany end tables, and painted chairs.

It has to be a pretty exceptional piece of wood or I would paint it. A mahogany chest that has no merit whatsoever could be very pretty if you painted green with lines—of course, all according to where it's going. Again, that takes experience: to do it properly and to do it with a sense of authority. It takes experience, no question about it. Most people today don't want to take the time.

DAVID WEBSTER You can paint it—you can do whatever. I think about people like Dorothy Draper and a few others before us. They had no fear about painting a Chippendale chair, painting it white, black, green—paint it whatever you want. They just had no concern about it. They just said be bold enough and do it.

BRIAN McCARTHY I think people, and this goes back to being afraid of trying things, when they go to dealers are afraid to ask questions because they don't want to look stupid. The only way people are going to learn is by asking questions. I think the dealers by and large love someone who is curious about a piece. Let's face it: most of these guys, whether they are selling old or new, are buying what they like. So if you're interested in buying it and you want to ask questions they are going to be equally interested in sharing whatever information they have.

LIBBY CAMERON Furniture is one of the more personal elements in decorating as people respond to styles of furniture and finishes so instantly and emphatically. They may have pieces that they have been given or inherited, or pieces that they have found along the way, all of which have meaning for different reasons. I try to put emotions aside when figuring out what goes where; furniture needs to be thought out and considered carefully. It's about balance, scale, and suitability.

I still have pieces that I found and loved when I first saw them thirty years ago, and have made them my own with a fresh coat of paint, new knobs, a different top—whatever. What you buy should be bought on instinct, because you're drawn by it. Never buy a piece just because you need something in that spot; that is how a house loses its soul.

COLOR

One of the most important decisions a person makes when putting together a room is what colors one will choose. Dorothy Draper was Sister's mother's first cousin, part of the Tuckerman family, and although very different in many ways, they both had an extremely confident approach to color, which characterized their work. In Draper's enchanting (and totally informative book) *Decorating Is Fun*, she begins her color chapter (aptly entitled "Color—Your Magic Wand") with the proclamation:

> *I wish there were one word in the English language that meant exciting, frightfully important, irreplaceable, deeply satisfying, basic, thrilling, all at once. I need that word to tell you how much your awareness of color means to you in decorating. It is the rock on which your house is built.*

Some people have an intrinsic sense of what colors will work together. Like a great chef, they throw in the fresh spices at the end of the stew that make it distinctive. They can't explain it as they work on instinct. My grandmother was a natural with color, which appeared to me to be her instinctive talent combined with her lack of fear. When Robert Jackson, the fabled decorative artist, came to Maine for a week of frenzied painting on the Summer House, he and Sister concocted the most brilliant painting schemes based on a series of quick consultations, probably lasting all of twenty minutes. He painted all of the floors in the old Maine house: apple green for the living room, red for one of the guest rooms, orange for the card room, and on it went. What is now my bathroom is painted a brilliant deep blue. He then covered the blue with little bouquets of multicolored wildflowers. The contrast of the old four-legged white tub against the brilliant blue is wonderful and surprising for a bathroom in a Maine cottage. He finished the week with two masterpieces—the dazzling

LIBBY CAMERON'S LIVING ROOM HAS A VARIETY OF PATTERNS AND TEXTURES. THE PYRAMID-SHAPED BOOKCASES FLANK A PAIR OF FRENCH DOORS. SISTER PARISH DESIGN'S "SERENDIPITY" FABRIC IS USED FOR THE CURTAINS, AND YELLOW "CAMPBELL" COVERS AN ELLIS CHAIR.

swirl of primary colors on the linoleum floor in the kitchen and the beautiful chinoiserie trompe l'oeil that goes up the stairs. Both are signatures of the Summer House.

Sister was a childhood friend of Howard Johnson and claimed that she was responsible for the famous orange/aqua combination his restaurants featured. Knowing her, this was probably an exaggeration, but it made for an amusing story. Once, when a magazine asked her to invent a dessert, she came up with chocolate jello, never a big hit, but the rich color was probably what she was after. She said if you put together any random bunch of flowers they would always be pretty—there were no color "mistakes in nature." Her genius was her boldness and how somehow, even with the strongest hues, one always felt comforted by her rooms. She said her favorite color was pink, but she used every color combination you can imagine. Many times she was drawn toward deep aubergines, blues, and reds for background colors, and then she shifted to the palest pinks and beiges. You couldn't point to one color scheme that she was known for. Many decorators look to their clients' taste in clothes. Hers were always appropriate. Black for night, pastels in summer. Children should always be dressed in the most appropriate colors. A purple and pink print dress on a three-year-old would be heresy for her.

She was bold in the exterior colors she used as well. When I was young she owned five houses in Maine. She basically collected them to install her children and grandchildren in and also added one for her in the winter. They were known by their colors. Aunt D.B. was in the "Brown House," a Victorian house painted shiny chocolate brown with bright white trim. Albert Hadley was the original owner and chose the color to look like the creosote on a dark brown telephone pole. Uncle Harry was in "the Barn," which was attached to the Brown House and was also originally owned by Albert and had the famous all-white hayloft/party room. It, too, was painted the creosote color. In the winter she was in the "Red House," a little cottage close to town, which she painted a brilliant red and also trimmed in white. In addition there was the "Town House," close to town, and the "Summer House," on the water. Both were painted yellow. Painting a house white would never occur to her. That would be too boring. Despite the flashy sound of these colors, they just totally fit the houses and enhanced whatever architectural details the houses had.

In his book *Billy Baldwin Decorates,* Billy notes a few rules of thumb about color that Sister practiced as well: strong or dark walls are better with a shiny finish, white goes well in any finish, soft colors and pastels look best in a matte finish, and no matter what color the walls are make all the woodwork and ceilings off-white. His concluding words on color sum up what we should all keep in mind when getting bogged down with color choices:

> But I find I am more concerned with seeing colors harmonize than with making sure they match. I sometimes wonder why so many decorators sit in wholesale houses leafing through swatch after swatch trying to find a precise match. I'd much prefer some other color—a variation on one of the colors in the print, for instance, or a blend of two colors. If you are timid about trying anything so daring as a not-matching color, just think for a moment of a summer garden against the sky. Not one color matches any other, and yet, can you think of anything more soul satisfying?

—SUSAN BARTLETT CRATER

THE POWER of COLOR

If you get it right the first time, there's no need for change.

ELEANOR MCMILLEN BROWN, *McMillen Inc.*

Ultimately, in my heart of hearts, colorful rooms are more exciting for me.

MILES REDD

WILLIAM HODGINS Mrs. Parish would shock you with her use of some of the colors that I would never have thought of or have put together. She was a great teacher without meaning to be a teacher. It seemed that she would just pick things out of the air, but that wasn't so. She would spot what she liked and pull it in. Like when she painted those drawing rooms of hers that eggplant. She did it. She was always sure that she was right. That was kind of interesting, too. I don't remember that it ever happened that she thought the color was wrong after it was done, or ever changing it. She was strong in a most kind of ladylike way. Most of the time it was ladylike, anyway. It always seemed to me, even in the power struggles, she was Madam.

LIBBY CAMERON I was spellbound by Mrs. Parish's use of color and her total lack of fear. She was absolutely brilliant in the way she used color and combined colors along with patterns upon patterns. She never seemed to think twice about pulling the least dominant color out of a fabric or out of a painting in a room. We worked on a house in Newport together and the client had always loved pink. Mrs. Parish and I put several tones of pinks, bright pinks, in the schemes for her house. It was consequently very bright and happy and

THE BOOKCASES IN BROOKE ASTOR'S LIBRARY ARE FRAMED IN BRASS AND THE WALLS ARE LACQUERED IN A DEEP, DARK RED, CREATING A WONDERFUL FRAMEWORK FOR HER LATE HUSBAND'S BOOK COLLECTION.

clear; all of the ceilings were painted a pale pink, and intermixed with the pinks were beiges and browns and creams—not what you would expect for a summer house facing east, done in the eighties. It was serene and unexpected.

I remember sitting in Albert's office and he asked me to visualize something. He said, "Imagine a rowboat with its ribs and seats and blocks of wood by the oarlocks on the inside, and on the outside hull, the piece of wood that goes across the back and up the point of the front. Now imagine if you painted the actual hull itself red inside and out, and if all of the other pieces I mentioned like the seats, the oarlock blocks, and the ribs were painted black." I thought about it and envisioned it as best I could. A minute later, he said, "Okay, now envision it in the opposite way—black hull inside and out, with red seats, oarlock blocks, and ribs." It was a fascinating moment for me and a revelation—the beginning of envisioning how colors work in such different ways. It was a lesson for my imagination that I will never forget.

ALBERT HADLEY There is an interesting color story about an outstanding room that Sis and I were responsible for. It started in London during one of our buying trips there. As we left one of our favorite shops I noticed that she was carrying a small package, and when I inquired about it, her answer was simply, "You shall see."

When we returned to New York, we were told that Mrs. William Paley had made an appointment to come to the offices to discuss work to be done in their new Fifth Avenue apartment. Naturally, we were surprised, as well as pleased, at the thought of working on a project with the Paleys, but at the same time, we knew that a prominent French firm was already engaged in work there.

Mrs. Paley arrived at our office a few days later and explained that much of the work in the apartment had been completed, but the drawing room was yet to be addressed. As our very agreeable and animated session wound down, there was no question that we had the job. But wait! As our client prepared to leave, Sis produced the casually wrapped package from our London jaunt and offered it to her. I don't know which of us—Mrs. Paley or myself—was more surprised when we saw the contents. It was a small nineteenth-century beadwork pillow, quite beautiful in detail and with the message "Welcome Babe"! Sis's only remark was, "I knew that you would come someday."

When Sis and I arrived at the apartment, we were pleased to find a beautifully proportioned pair of doors opening from the entrance hall into the drawing room. Three tall windows on the opposite wall overlooked Central Park. The renowned French firm Jansen had installed simple, quite beautiful eighteenth-century-style boiserie inspired by one of Bill Paley's favorite rooms in Paris. The room needed work, but the possibilities were great. Much work was to be done before one could even think of color. We needed to consider their impressive art collection as well as some eighteenth-century French furniture, plus a fabulous ten-paneled red lacquer Coromandel screen—all to be used. The design process flowed; however, a final color scheme for the space was not established. As work progressed, Bill Paley eventually called a meeting to address the subject.

The four of us met in the white prime-coated space just as Jansen had left it. Paley asked his wife her preference for the final color and finish for the impressive paneling. Poor Babe, she didn't know where to start. She glanced at me and I hesitated but finally voiced my opinion, which was for a classically white room with possibly gold accents. I was thinking of the art collection as well as the Coromandel screen. Babe agreed with me, adding that she wished to have a light room as a background for evening entertaining. Bill looked slightly amused at the idea and slightly nodding his head turned to Sis for her opinion. Without a moment's hesitation, she very authoritatively proclaimed, "Taxi cab yellow!"

Bill immediately broke into gales of laughter, happily repeating, "Yes, yes, yes, that's it!" Obviously there erupted more discussion, but more obviously Sis had won the game. That was just the beginning of a great challenge that we all became excited about, and I accepted the responsibility of getting the job done. Taxi cab yellow—okay—but not so fast! Working with our crew of painters—artisans, really—the goal was "the color" first of all, but to add subtlety and quality various techniques were used including shadings and glazes. The finished effect was one of lustrous, glowing yellow. No cabbie could have been more pleased! The drive had been a great success and the destination was clearly in sight. A finished room of rare distinction. In the end, the color and the techniques used merely become a suitably animated background—and rightly so.

MARIO BUATTA I think the most exciting thing in life is color. Having color around you is a mood setter. I was brought up in a room that was basically a bland color and I hated it. I found it depressing. I couldn't wait to have a color bedroom. So what did I do when I was sixteen? I created a dark brown bedroom with a red interior closet and maple bedroom furniture. I had hunter green carpeting wall to wall and red-and-green-plaid curtains. I was starting to collect when I was eleven—Early American antiques basically and then I got into English. I love color—in my apartment on 62nd Street I had bright pineapple yellow walls, and when you came in from the gray city you felt like you were in a sunny, happy place. I think from the time you are born you need to be in a room full of color. I don't understand these rules like a blue room for a boy. Why can't a boy have yellow? It makes them happy. You wake up in the morning and you want to be happy. You don't want to be glum.

I may go overboard on color. I think Sister went overboard with color, but it was beautiful. When I went to her house in Maine she only let me see it from one corner. She wouldn't let me into the other rooms. Did you ever hear that story? I stayed there for a week back in 1972 with Dorothy Robinson, who was a guest of Harry's, and we stayed in the Brown House. She invited me up for a week, and immediately after we arrived Dorothy said, "Mrs. Parish wants to see you," and I said, "No, I'll call her tomorrow." "No, no, she wants to see you now," she said. So I said all right and called her. I said, "Guess who's on the island," and she said, "I know. You've got to come over right away." So we went by for tea and she sat me in that Aiken sofa in the dining area. When I got up to leave an hour later and said, "Oh it's such a pretty house," she replied, "This is all you're going to see," and she opened the door and pushed me out. It was very funny. But she had an incredible sense of color. It was amazing. John Fowler, Nancy Lancaster—they had it and that's where I learned. Sister was part of the same school. They were all pals. John could put a color on the wall and it was just amazing.

SUSAN BARTLETT CRATER One of my favorite writers on design is Mark Hampton. I always felt you could learn more from talking with him about decorating than taking ten years of classes at any design school. He literally missed nothing. In a wonderful essay on color in his book, *Mark Hampton on Decorating*, he sums up Albert Hadley's amazing grasp of color and his use of white in the hayloft room in the Barn in Maine. The beauty of the hayloft room that Albert created stems in part from the cathedral-like architecture of the room, but it also comes from the subtlety of the all-white scheme he chose to decorate it in. Mark provides a wonderful description of Albert's treatment of the room and the power of his choices.

The no-color philosophy is applicable in a broad range of decorating and can be practiced in widely divergent situations. Take, for instance, two rooms created by Albert Hadley. The barn room had all of the characteristics that make you want to turn every pretty old barn into a house. There were old rough beams and great open spaces. A tall window, reminiscent of an artist's studio (another fantasy mood I always love), provided light and a broad view over fields and woods, the sort of view barns are supposed to have. The floors, walls, and ceiling were different tones and textures of white and off-white. The upholstered furniture was covered in a pale cotton twill that was neither beige nor cream. A beautifully carved trophy of a stag's head with real antlers was whitewashed and hung over the mantel. A few pieces were painted white and others were left in straw or natural bamboo. There were witty references to every possible twentieth-century phase of interior design. Living together in contented harmony were a 1950s standing lamp in chrome and steel, a Louis XVI bench covered in Dutch East Indies batik, Lucite tables, angular sofas like Syrie Maugham's and Jean Michel Frank's, Regency bamboo, and even a calfskin rug. The aim was not to achieve a flashy opulence with calla lilies in goldfish bowls. It was to create a summery mood of carefree simplicity, lightness, and comfort in addition to an amusing stylishness based on a broad collection of furniture. The vehicle for this ambitious objective was the no-color scheme.

—MARK HAMPTON

ALBERT HADLEY In the early days of Parish-Hadley I would often drive my sporty Sunbeam convertible to Maine, to spend time with Sis and Harry Parish, their family and friends. It was a demanding trip, often defying speed limits in order to catch the four o'clock ferry to the island where the Parishes had family property dating from Sis's childhood. I loved being there.

There was a charming, small Victorian house on the road near Dark Harbor, the area where the Parishes lived, that was one of my favorite houses along the way. Beyond the house, on the edge of a cleared meadow, was a beautiful small barn with an ample hayloft above the animal stalls below. The property was owned by a friend—Ruth—Mrs. Marshall Field, whose own house was beyond the meadow and the grove of pine trees on the water side of the island. Knowing my interest in the property and her own desire for additional accommodations for a growing family, Sis persuaded Ruth to sell! I was thrilled.

Friends and neighbors were all attentive and curious about our plans for the place. Inside, the house was well arranged with a series of modest-size rooms on two floors. Sis and I set about creating colorful, simple rooms. I also really loved the old barn. There were a couple of stalls for animals downstairs and some doors that looked out onto the field. We created a bedroom and a bathroom, a small sitting room, and a kitchen downstairs. When you went up the steps you came to the second floor, originally a giant hayloft, where we put in a huge window, so it was all the beams and those ceilings that went up twenty feet, and this great view. The entire room was all white and gray and it was a great room to be in with wonderful light. It was very Swedish in a way.

But the real point of this is what happened outside. When spring came, it was time to paint both house and barn. There was much discussion about color and I thought I'd won the battle. The painters employed were dismayed

ALBERT HADLEY USED
SUBTLE VARIATIONS OF
WHITES ON THE WALLS,
FLOORS, AND BEAMS,
WHICH CREATED A
DRAMATIC BACKGROUND
IN THIS OLD RENOVATED
BARN.

and suggested—actually insisted—that work begin on the back of the house,
leaving the barn until the very last. Curiosity was mounting and passing cars
came to a near halt while some friends actually ventured to the back of the
house to see what was going on. Here is where I should tell you that most of

the houses on the island were white or gray or some other pale color. Two of the Parish houses were painted almost canary yellow and the so-called Red House, just down the road, was bright red—all with white trim. There was such a commotion about the color I had chosen that the fear of being banned from the island hung heavily overhead.

As spring unfolded, trees fresh with new leaves framed the house and the meadow was dotted with blossoms. Moods changed and tensions eased—slightly. It wasn't until the job was finished, the painters gone, that one could view the little house with its Victorian detail, gleaming fresh with warm white paint. Its clapboard siding was undeniably beautiful in its rich, creosote color—the color matched to an ancient telephone pole—rich black-brown. Even the natives expressed approval and I was happily "at home" to friends and neighbors. I might add in closing that the house and barn have maintained the "creosote color" over the years, blending very successfully into the landscape.

LIBBY CAMERON Color can make a room come alive and can transform an anemic room into a room of strength and character. The colors don't always have to be bright and strong, or overwhelming; they can be subtle and even be seen in tones of wood. There is nothing prettier than limed or pickled wood—it is a wonderful background for almost any color scheme and has a lovely warmth and depth.

Contrasts in color tones are wonderful because colors end up playing off each other, creating an interesting mix and liveliness. Color on a ceiling adds an unexpected dimension. I have done several ceilings wallpapered with gold or silver tea paper, and have also used tea paper on walls. Recently I used gold tea paper on the ceiling of a dining room that has red walls; the effect is quite wonderful and dramatic. I have always heard that red is a stimulating color and promotes lively conversation. The combination of the red and gold sounds garish but it's not: the curtains are cream and gold and the room is lined with books so the red recedes and the light bounces off the ceiling—the textures and colors of the books settle the room.

Years ago I worked on a dining room with Mrs. Parish in Washington. The color of the dining room began with a pair of curtains, which I found at Elinor Merrell's shop in New York. She had the most wonderful collection of antique textiles and just happened to have this pair of curtains that were in immaculate condition. There was a wonderful marine blue in the border of the curtains, which was the basis for the walls. Painters worked for weeks trying to get the depth and hue that that blue had. Coats of lacquer were applied over a glaze. Depending on the light and time of day, the walls changed color. In the room, there was an orangey-red chinoiserie armoire and a multicolored needlepoint rug with blues and corals; all of the contrasting colors together were a feast for the eyes.

BRIAN McCARTHY Clients do not always understand the importance of the play of color off of color and how important that is to a space. You can't be so rigid and literal. The eye blends color naturally so that what on paper may not look perfect in actuality is all going to come together—assuming you aren't making a trainwreck in the process. It is trial and error. I tell my clients that decorating is not a science. You have to begin with an open mind, and you have to go into it with an idea that you are going to make some mistakes along the way and that you have to suck it up. It doesn't mean you have to start over again, but you have to be willing to say, okay, this color didn't work perfectly, so let's work on it to get it right. Some of the shelter magazines have terrified people into believing you shouldn't use color since there is so little color you see being used. Which is a little like what the fashion world was doing five years ago when it was the whole Prada-Gucci thing and everybody wanted to buy Prada and Gucci—it was like going to a Catholic girl's school when you had to put on a uniform.

I love color used judiciously. I think because I have gotten so into art I like to have background color, but I don't necessarily want it to overshadow the art. That's not to say that I am not going to use strong color. We just did this turquoise lacquer library in California for a client, and it's an amazing background for works on paper or for paintings. You have to be bold. The way I did the chocolate brown on this ceiling creates this sandwich effect for the room and gives it a strength, without taking away from the lightness of the room. Too many people overlook ceilings. I think ceilings are forgotten and that they are very important to a space.

DANIEL ROMUALDEZ Contrasts can be great. If everything is a pastel it can be a little blah. So it's nice to throw something different in and see how it looks. It's almost like putting together an outfit. A lot of times that's what I use with my clients—the getting-dressed analogy. Because everyone gets dressed in the morning and everyone makes design decisions and color decisions and accessory decisions. I try to bring about their style or what they want and I really take a lot of cues from what they wear at the meetings. Sometimes you meet them and they have just come from dropping off the kids or they are off to lunch or on their way to dinner, and you just sort of factor all of this in—is she going to look great in her living room? It has to be in her style. If she is at the beach in a bathing suit, she should be able to walk into her living room or into her entry hall and look wonderful. You have to use flattering colors. In bedrooms, for example, most people want soothing colors. Very rarely does someone want a red, orange, or yellow bedroom. With a dining room, it is absolutely important to have a flattering color because people are sitting there in candlelight.

In my apartment there is a mix. One of my favorite rooms to sit in is a pale room with a pale floor and pale furniture. It's soothing and happy, especially in the winter because it's usually dark out. Everyone thinks of a light room as a summer room or a beach room. So you have this sense of light when it's kind of dreary outside. But at the same time, and I did one for myself, I have a black library. I have ended up doing a lot of very dark or black rooms for my clients. I learned from Sir Edward Lutyens that black (because he did a room painted black and I read this discussion of it) has really all colors in it. In his room, he had a green floor and a Chinese lacquer cabinet and some yellow curtains. In my library I tried that. I figured what better to do than black, because of all the different colors of the book spines. Then I put in this beautiful rug I bought years before with amazing colors—apple green, hot pink, sky blue—as opposed to doing a black-and-white room. It didn't become this Darth Vader–slick room. Darker colors make a room look bigger, but they are a harder sell because it's counterintuitive. A dark color makes the walls recede. Of course it also depends on the lighting and the kind of paint finish.

MILES REDD I like living rooms and dining rooms to be rich colors, and I like bedrooms and bathrooms to be sort of airy and fresh. I like waking up to something that is clutter-free and fresh. I think all colors go together ultimately. The second someone says, oh, that's a hideous combination, I'll say I will show you an example of it in nature. I think it all works together. I like using a warmer palette in living rooms. It depends on where it is, but I am a great lover of everything. I always think the second you start to say something is a bad idea, someone will do it in a great and unusual way. So I never want to be the naysayer. At the same time, as a decorator you are hired to be the editor. You are hired to be the one who says I think that's not a great decision or a good choice.

A LARGE-SCALE WALLPAPER PRINT CREATES THE EFFECT OF A MURAL. BRACKETS AND MIRRORS ENHANCE THE WALLPAPER.

But I always tell people to go stronger rather than weaker. There is always this middle range of insipid tepid colors. I say go for a rich color.

DANIEL ROMUALDEZ Usually if we are doing color it's because my client wants color. I try to push them to do a more interesting version of the color. I remind them that it's not going to be an all-intense-yellow room. You have to imagine it will be broken up. A lot of times, if they are nervous about color, we put it in a room that they walk through quickly as opposed to a room they hang out in. Some people are attracted to the idea of color, but they are afraid of it. So I'll say let's put it in a hallway—it can be a nice break between all the neutral rooms.

When you are doing a strong color or an unusual color, you don't want the client to say, I can't take it. I learned that when I was doing the first house I did with my partner. We had a couple of dark rooms and I painted one light yellow and one light green and after that, when it was furnished, he never questioned me again. It was amazing to see someone have such a reaction. It was a good lesson to learn. When there is a color that is controversial, I make sure I am there when the client sees it for the first time.

EMMA BURNS Sometimes I say we don't need to talk about the colors until we have resolved how the room is going to work. I might have an idea of the colors that we should be using. Some of my clients have very strong ideas about color as well, and I know that because I discover this when I talk to them in the beginning. I work a lot with a French client and she is very passionate about a particular pink, which is actually the most fantastic color, an amazing background. It is so sophisticated and it can be used in so many different kinds of contexts. So if I am working for her I know that that color is going to be in the equation. Clothes tell a huge deal about people. It is something I always look at. There is a theory that the more well dressed the clients, the less attractive their home will be because people will focus on one thing or another!

USING COLOR

I had this white-painted apartment in New York and David Hicks came around for a drink. I asked him, "Oh, do you think I should paint the walls a color?" David said, "My dear boy, you know it's very nice to have white walls, if you've got something good to put on them." So I thought okay we better paint it a color. Obviously if someone has a Picasso over the fireplace everything is going to look good, including them. PETER DUNHAM

ALBERT HADLEY In our conversations about color, the question of the color beige came up. There are many shades of this beige, just as there are in all colors, therefore one should be specific in recommendations. The darker tones can be just as demanding as any other color, while in its lighter application—often termed "warm white"—it is an agreeable background color, often employed with great success.

Do we see too many interiors where this neutral shade is preferred? Maybe, maybe not. Color triggers a very personal response and rules of right and wrong are to be addressed very carefully. There are many of those who feel more comfortable and less challenged by life in surroundings that lack visual stimulants. Perhaps the majority. Who knows?

BUNNY WILLIAMS I, of course, love color. Color is something that I have found that I can live with better when I have a contrast—it's sort of a yin and yang. If I am going to use a very strong color, I have to have a neutral color with it. That neutral color might be mossy green or something that is just not a really strong color. I get tired of (mainly because I have been through it several times) saturated primary colors all together. I love hot pink, orange, turquoise, but I tend to like to mix colors like these with something that is more of a neutral color because then I think it is more interesting. If I am doing a color scheme, I may use a strong color, but there will be some faded colors with it so that

there is juxtaposition. It then becomes more timeless. It doesn't become dated. For a while color was all very intense, then color got all washed out and it was supposed to be old granny, then all that becomes trendy and people get tired of it. If you love color you will get less tired of it if you learn how to neutralize it. I am not going to have a bright orange sofa, but I might have orange pillows on a neutral sofa. The hotter the color, the smaller amounts I will use in a room.

If you stand back and you look from room to room to room, you should see one of the colors in one room and then in the other rooms. You should have a flow. I think you want each room to feel different, but there needs to be an incredible sort of harmony. The space will look bigger. If you have a pink room and a yellow room and a blue room it becomes very choppy. If you want to have a yellow room and the next room has some yellow in it—it makes the spaces look bigger and it leads you from one space to another.

I am always thinking when I do a room of the scheme in the next room. Often the living room might be lighter and the family room next to it will be darker—at least in tonality so they feel different—but there will probably be some of the same colors, just much darker versions of them. So you can make rooms feel different by having a room with a light color next to one with a deeper color.

PETER DUNHAM I think one of the great tools we have is color and pattern. The minute someone takes that away from me and wants something with no pattern or color, I keep on trying to push and push. I'll say, okay, let's try high-gloss lacquer—or let's try something else. I'm not one who wants pattern and color everywhere, but I do want it to use in certain places. In a real dump of a room I'll want to go crazy with it.

I don't really know if I have a set answer for what colors work best in specific rooms. I do a lot of things, like if someone has bright blue eyes, I'll always make

CARLETON VARNEY RECENTLY DESIGNED A FRONT HALL IN A HOUSE IN DALLAS, TEXAS, THAT WAS ORIGINALLY DECORATED BY DOROTHY DRAPER. MR. VARNEY'S EXUBERANT USE OF COLOR AND FLOWERS AND SENSE OF SCALE ARE ALL TRADEMARKS OF THE DOROTHY DRAPER LOOK.

the room about their eyes. Because it makes them more attractive. If you have a headboard and you've got blue eyes and you make a blue headboard, to me it's like a magnet—it makes them shine. So I do a lot of that. I think it really depends on the circumstances—how big is the room, what is it, what's in it? I did a room that I found just suffocating for this young girl from New York. She said, "I want you to paint it all maroon." So then I built up a lot of fabrics that had maroon in them because I couldn't bear to just paint the walls maroon.

Usually, I like something that is kind of light and airy. A sense of breeziness and light and airy is healthy to me. I'll tend to go that way. Except when something is like a dark cavern. In that case, then just make it more of a cavern. If a room is dark and dingy, I'll just take it further that way.

JANE CHURCHILL I am a blue person. People always say that. The thing about blue—Jim Smart told me and he is a fantastic painter—is that when you mix the paint you put a tube of red in it because it takes out that look of the inside of a swimming pool.

MARIO BUATTA Rose Cummings used silver. I remember when I was a student working at Altman's, we used to go to her house on Saturdays—a whole bunch of us—and move furniture for her. It was across from the Museum of Modern Art. Afterward, she would give us dinner, which would invariably be stewed tomatoes and tuna fish casserole. The stewed tomatoes were always all runny and the peas had no color. She would arrive with this silver tray and we would all be sitting in the mirrored dining room with a blue ceiling and mirrored tabletop and I think the chairs were red. One night she slipped and the tray went flying. She just said thank goodness we cleaned today, and she put it all back together. We had to sit there and eat it all.

Rose was a woman who had incredible color sense. Her colors were purple, blue, green—all sorts of gem colors, jewel colors. She was fascinating. Sister knew her very well. She used to shop at Rose's all the time and they loved each other. The first time I met her I was working at Altman's and I came up to number 515, the building on Madison where all the decorating shops were. I walked into her shop and she was sweeping. I went in and she said, "Out!" I didn't even get into the shop and she said what do you want? She brushed me out with her broom. Two years later I went in for some samples and she was sort of grumpy. I came back two months later because I had been sick and had to be operated on. So I brought back the samples late and didn't order anything. I said I am sorry I had your samples out for so long. Oh, young man, she said, you look terrible. I had lost so much weight. So she sat me down at the window—and she was here and I was there—and she opens a drawer and pulls out a teapot and cup and starts pouring. People going by saw this lady having a cup of tea, but it was bourbon.

JOSIE McCARTHY I just did a young girl's apartment, and we made it very modern and used a very simple but dramatic color scheme. We did a white rug and we made white lacquer furniture for the room. She wanted it modern and hot pink. I did these hot pink lamps that were the most expensive thing in the room from John Boone. We used great white fabric. I think you can get a look going with just simple things and a simple color scheme.

SUZANNE TUCKER I love when I get a client who loves color and isn't afraid of it. Most people are afraid of color and want to play it safe. It's a bit like looking at a restaurant menu where there might be things that are challenging, like sushi, and you don't want to quite go there. If I can push people into understanding color and using color, I always think that is ultimately really enjoyable. I find that a lot of what influences people's color preferences are the shelter magazines. So what the magazines publish is what people think they are supposed to have.

A lot of the trend in the last six to seven years has been very neutral—white and beiges are very safe. I have a theory about that: after 9/11 people wanted colors that were safe. They wanted things that were not challenging. I think the trend now is going back to more color and I encourage that because I think color can make a home an individual space versus one that looks like every other house.

I always go for flattering colors. Flattering meaning that when you have incandescent light they are flattering to one's coloring. Green is a challenging color for dining rooms. You definitely need the warmth of candlelight to avoid that green cast. Face it, you're sitting down and you are looking at each other for a period of time over dinner and you want people to look well. Even an apple green will not look good because there is too much blue in it. So candlelight is really important in balancing that. The only color that I really personally don't use is mauve. It's a weird color.

Any color can be used as long as you understand lighting and how to use lighting in a room. Even with the most flattering beautiful color in a room, if the lighting is bad, people are going to look ghoulish and the room is going to look flat. I love to mix my own colors for the paint and add a complexity to the pigments, which then changes throughout the day.

It's funny, when I was interviewed recently for *House Beautiful* on colors for brunettes, I thought to myself, certainly that whole concept of what you look best in does apply. I look more at the skin tone because skin tone can't change. You can put contacts in and change your eye color. Hair color doesn't count unless you are a redhead and you're going to stay a redhead. Definitely redheads look great in certain color rooms like green—and sort of celadon blue rooms—these make redheads just look stunning because they have sort of a peach color skin tone.

Blonds can go a lot of ways. Actually one of the funniest and personally educational experiences that I ever had dealing with color was with a male client. He was recently divorced and he wanted to change the house and finish things. He was a super-successful financier. When I asked him what his favorite colors were, he went apoplectic. He could not answer my question. I realized that he was struggling with this concept of favorite and I tried to phrase it in

BRUNSCHWIG & FILS'S "SHELF LIFE" WALLPAPER FRAMES A COLLECTION OF NECKTIES BESIDE A GENTLEMAN'S DRESSER.

different ways, and then suddenly I said, "Would you mind indulging me? If you can go to your dressing room and bring me your favorite ties, we can talk about this." He said okay and I could hear him upstairs rummaging around, and he came down with twenty ties and threw them on the coffee table, like a golden retriever bringing back a ball. I started asking him about his ties; what he liked about this tie, what he liked about that tie, and we figured it out.

It was interesting to find a vehicle to get to that person's sense of color and what he liked. The most basic question—what's your favorite color—he didn't go there. Of course if he had asked me a question about the market I would have done exactly the same thing—frozen.

MARTHA ANGUS I'm always sizing up what my clients are wearing. I look at their eye color and their hair color, and those are always their favorite colors. My clients with black hair can't get enough black furniture and my pale clients like Gustavian things, pale things. With most people you look at their eye color and that's their favorite color.

PAUL VINCENT WISEMAN I don't think there are rights and wrongs. Think of all the blond blue-eyed ladies you know and how they resonate in certain color ranges. I have this great Puerto Rican client. We did her house in Hawaii and she said, "Now baby, when you go shopping for my fabrics, I want you to put headphones on and play only salsa music. If you show me anything beige, it's your kneecaps." Her house was in *Architectural Digest* a couple of months ago. It's fabulous. It was packed with colors like pink and yellow and it's where she resonates. Their main house is really beautiful.

CATHY KINCAID You know I tell this story because it is about my first job, straight after college. I had gotten my degree and my internship was with two designers in Fort Worth named Joseph Minton and David Corley. They were really popular in the seventies and eighties, so it was a big deal for me. They needed somebody so they hired me right then. Of course they were busy and Joe

JEFFREY BILHUBER HAS CREATED AN ORANGE BACKDROP FOR THE CENTER
TABLE, WHICH SERVES AS A DESK AS WELL AS A DINING TABLE.

came in one day and said, here, do this room for me. Pull every fabric that you
can and a couple of great carpets and put it together. As you can imagine, I was
scared to death and I matched it all just perfectly. I got this great background
and I got fabric that had flowers. I matched it just perfectly and I was so proud
of myself. He came in, looked at me, and said that looks cheap. I died. I said,

"Oh no." He said, "Don't match it like that—it's terrible. It's dull and soft." Then he said you'll get the idea—go with the gray and just don't match. When he walked out of the room, I was about to cry. I thought, well, I have got to keep my job. So I went and I pulled everything and I did what he told me to do. He came in and he said okay that looks better, good. I filed that away.

It's not as if you have to have blue in every single room. If blue is your favorite color, as it tends to be most people's, use it. All women want blue and white porcelain for some reason. Some people say keep the same woodwork throughout the house. I don't believe in that, but you have to have some sort of a connector. A lot of times we use three shades of white in an entryway, and from there you take the darkest shade and go into the kitchen for all of your woodwork in there. Then you take a color from your kitchen and move that into the family room, if that's the way the house works. Not that it all has to be the same, but as you go from one room to the next you feel there is continuity. That you are not just creating a new scheme every time.

CARLETON VARNEY Dorothy Draper would go from office to office and walk around the desks, and if it didn't have her okay—D.D. on it—it didn't happen. She would say, "Show me nothing that looks like gravy." So there was never anything gray, beige, or cream. Dorothy Draper lived in the world of magical color. She would paint a room navy blue or sable brown or garnet because she knew that in a smaller space, the thing was to make it cozy. She never did anything in an understated way.

I always say that there are certain things that are God-given. I had Ethel Merman as a client and she never had any voice lessons, but she could sing to the top balcony. The thing that made her special was that Ethel had perfect diction, so that when she sang a song you knew the story. Most of these stars today garble and gook and so forth; they are so amplified you don't even know what they are saying.

Dorothy Draper was blessed with a vision of color that no one in this industry has ever had since. She also represented something this generation knows nothing about—and that is glamour. Dorothy's period was El Morocco, she created public places with red velvet banquettes and wonderful murals, places where people would come and look beautiful. Dorothy was all about beauty.

SUSAN BARTLETT CRATER Being adventuresome with color, like scale, is challenging and decorators really have to exert their authority to give clients the confidence to use it. The irony is that when you remember a truly exceptional room, it is usually a wonderful color that comes to mind. It can be the main color of the room taken from the fabric or the walls or it can be one lone object that stands out. Sister said every room should have some gold in it, and Slim Keith once told me every room should have something red in it. These catalyst colors bring everything together or spice everything up. The other thing about choosing color is that different cities have absolute favorite colors. We learned this with selling our fabrics in different markets. Los Angeles and San Francisco, for example, lean toward more muted colors; in New York anything goes.

TODD ROMANO As I have gotten older and, dare I say, more mature, I understand that colors can come from so many different sources. When I was younger and probably less experienced my idea of color was you buy a can of red paint and you dip two cats in it, you let them chase each other around the room, and you have this bright red room. I just did a house in South Texas, very modern and very marvelous—U shaped—and one of the first things they asked me is what colors do I see? I said it's funny because I don't see any colors. This house has walls of glass and looks out to the most beautiful lawns, garden, and trees, and I said, "There is your color, your color is outside. You don't need it inside." Color comes in whether it's a vase of flowers or a stack of books. I was attracted to pop art as a young child. I remember the first time I saw those Warhols and the strength of that color clearly made a huge impression on me. So I think that my love of color started as a child with my exposure to pop art.

CAROLYN ENGLEFIELD Donald Kaufman's book on color says, "The colors with which we surround ourselves in daily life affect us profoundly." And as with everything else, I believe that decorating and color is cyclical, too. There is a natural order in time and nature that provides us with change.

Remember back to the eighties when decorating was over the top. Opulence and abundance appeared to be the rule, not the exception. Rooms were full of color, pattern, tassels, and more trims than imaginable (not to mention the cost of all of the materials). That being said, in 1989 I was introduced to someone very special, who at the time had a very different point of view. His name is Roger Lussier. He owns a picture gallery and frame shop in Boston situated just above what was Apple Bartlett's shop, La Ruche. The Swedish furniture painter John Anderson introduced him as one of Boston's best-kept secrets, and I told him I must see his apartment. Upon entering the space I remember being so struck by his soft color palette of beautifully painted pale gray walls in the living room and soft apricot in the bedroom. Chalk white–painted furniture that combined with his eclectic mix of fine drawings, furniture, and accessories, including white export porcelain and an amazing collection of creamware. Not to mention an all-white porcelain dollhouse complete with white porcelain furniture.

The memory is of a perfectly edited apartment, refined by the pale color palette creating the perfect backdrop for the pale painted Swedish furniture and fine collection of unique accessories and antiques. The subtle accents of gold, gilt, and silver leaf on the accessories and furniture added a sparkling touch to the well-appointed room. The lasting impression was of someone who had great personal style. We knew who he was and how he wanted to live. He surrounded himself with all his favorite precious things, which he had been collecting for years. There was a perfect order to his place and the background colors set the tone down to the very last detail.

MATERIALS and TEXTURES

A few years after I started working at Parish-Hadley, Mrs. Parish moved from 960 Fifth to 920 Fifth Avenue. The new apartment needed quite a bit of work, and she put me in charge of running and organizing the renovation, along with Paul Engle, one of Parish-Hadley's architects. Mrs. Parish went to Maine for most of the summer so we were all under pressure to get it done so that she could move in the fall, but needless to say, it took longer than expected. Her intent was to bring everything she had from one apartment to the other, and reuse all of her living room furniture as it was. The new apartment was bigger, so she needed some new pieces—furniture and upholstery—but the important pieces she had and she knew long before anyone else exactly where those pieces would go and what the apartment would look like. That was one of the most magical times I had while working at Parish-Hadley, and one of the most intense; I had the most important client imaginable to keep happy.

Mrs. Parish had found two large decorative panels—I think they were from Arthur Smith's shop. They were chartreuse green fantasy Oriental panels, with pagodas and goats and people walking on tightropes suspended between pagodas in the panels. That was the starting point for her library. There was a coral orangey-pink color in the panels. Mrs. Parish said, "I want my library to be the color of lobster bisque." Temo Callahan came to the office from Clarence House to show us their new collection of wallpapers: there was a cream and barely off-white striped wallpaper that Mrs. Parish instantly loved for her new living room walls. Her old living room walls had at one point been a glossy aubergine, and later were wallpapered with a very pretty pale blue, cream, and gold stripe, so she had used quite a bit of color in her living rooms before. Since she planned to use her upholstery as it was, there was to be a lot of white in the new living room.

Well, months later, when it was done, moving day arrived. It poured, and

WALLPAPER ADDS A RUSTIC YET TEXTURED SURFACE THAT ENHANCES THE TREE PILASTERS IN THIS COUNTRY LIVING ROOM.

poured, and poured rain—all day long. The floors throughout the apartment had been pickled, so every speck of mud and dirt showed. There were a pair of gilt wood girandoles, which she insisted be carried the four blocks to the new apartment, for fear that the delicate garlands on the sides would break. Because of the weather, the move took hours longer than anticipated. Mrs. Parish stopped by just after lunch between meetings and was not very happy. I was a wreck and imagined that all her white silk damask upholstery would turn gray, if not black, in the rain. I worked with the movers until nine, went home, and returned by seven the next morning to start unpacking. Everything had stayed wrapped overnight; my dreams that night were nightmares—of black smudges and gray stains. Miraculously, every piece of upholstery survived without looking any worse for the wear. Mrs. Parish had a beautiful oval Aubusson rug, with the most wonderful jewel-tone colors in it—emerald greens, ruby reds, sapphire blues—it was the focus of her living room. The two sofas, a chaise longue, and the two upholstered armchairs were all in a white silk damask from Scalamandre, and the frame chairs were all covered in "Floral Bouquet," a beautiful chintz with a white background and multicolored flowers of the same jewel-tone colors as her rug. Most of the furniture was white and gold: the two lamps on either side of the big sofa opposite the fireplace were white ceramic; the Bouillotte lamps beside the fireplace were a gilt bronze with painted, striped metal shades; the tables had pieces of her ivory collection on them; there was a small, triangular red lacquer tiered table; and a multicolored throw across the bottom of the chaise. The gilt wood girandoles were at the far end of the room as you walked in, beside curtains of pale blue cotton taffeta with a cotton braid set in from the three-inch cotton fringe sewn at the edges of the curtains and valances. There were ruby red silk pillows on the two sofas and a striped antique needlepoint pillow in the middle of the biggest sofa. When that living room was put together and settled, the room did not feel too white by any means; it had more textures, variations of materials and sheen and a reflection of light, and more energy than I could ever have imagined. It was a beautiful, colorful yet serene, and very elegant room.

—LIBBY CAMERON

PAINT FINISHES
and TEXTURES

Always try the color out in the room. Even in England, where you think the light is gray wherever you go, it looks different in different places. It will look different in the country—it will look different in the north.

JANE CHURCHILL

LIBBY CAMERON During our meetings at Parish-Hadley we would discuss a house or apartment and what direction it should take. I would sit down with Albert, usually at the very end of the day, and go through the floor plan, and discuss the rooms and point of view the house should have. There was some basis from which he started—be it a rug or a painting or a "look" that someone wanted—and that's where the whole concept of the house was born. Some clients are very inarticulate at first about what it is they want, and they come with huge expectations that you are essentially going to be able to satisfy their every need, but they also change so much in the process. As they become more knowledgeable, they become more confident and challenge you more and more as time goes on, which is a good thing.

Albert was very academic and very precise and intellectual in the whole process, and there was definitely an organized way in which he went about doing things with drawings and elevations, whereas Mrs. Parish was very instinctive; she just knew if something would fit or not. It was just her instinct. With Albert, you would sit down and he would say, "I can see this being . . . "—he'd say whatever was on his mind. He used to talk about colors and textures, tobacco-colored linen is one he loved, so that would be the place where we would start and the whole room would evolve. He'd say he wanted to see some linen velvets, some textures, woven fabrics, and then something with some sheen, something with some polish, and he would mix it all up. There were enough things in the office—even things that the decorators had on their desks to mix in to see the

Mita Corsini Island

concept, like a door knocker I had on my desk that was a gilded tassel—and we would pull in things like that so that you would get a sense of what all the different materials would look like together; you would get a sense of the sheen versus the matte finish of something else, and the weight of a fabric and its texture and how it balances out a room.

KATHRYN IRELAND I always feel that a house has to have a certain flow. One room has got to connect to the next. You have to somehow keep a palette as you wind your way through. That doesn't mean that you can't have an orange bedroom and a musty brown library. I prefer that the walls are always quite quiet. My walls are quiet because I like to build on them. I start off with a blank canvas and just add on, layering colors and textures between the fabric and the carpet.

SUSAN BARTLETT CRATER I love to watch a room transformed when the wallpaper goes up. It can change its character entirely. Like many people, my love of wallpaper comes from the memories I have of wallpapered rooms from my childhood. Patterns and colors one associates with good memories can be imprinted on the mind the same way certain smells evoke the past. Anytime I smell mothballs I think of early June and summer houses. Often these memories evoke powerful associations and we repeat them later in houses of our own. In my Aunt D.B.'s house in Maine, Albert chose a simple white paper with a small gold print for the front hall. The crispness of the white and gold paper gave a modern fresh feeling to the entrance hall, which set off the inviting warmth of the pink sitting room next door. In designing the wallpapers for our wallpaper collection I think back to that crisp simple entrance that was such a pleasing tease to the rest of the house. My grandmother liked to use wallpaper borders a lot. She loved the English hand-blocked ones by Cole and Sons, which had ten colors and were almost like miniature floral paintings they

THIS BEDROOM HAS A WHIMSICAL FEEL GENERATED BY THE "SPRING CLOSE" WALLPAPER, WHICH ALSO ADDS HEIGHT TO THE ROOM.

A SEPIA-TONED MURAL
ADDS TRANQUILLITY TO
AN ENTRANCE HALL.
THE WALLS, DADO,
AND BASEBOARD
ARE ALL PAINTED IN
A FAUX FINISH. THE
UPPER PORTION OF
THE MURAL IS PAINTED
IN RECTANGULAR
SECTIONS, WHICH ADDS
MORE TEXTURE, DEPTH,
AND INTEREST.

were so beautiful. Libby's house in Larchmont is a feast of wonderful wallpapers that beguile you from room to room. Unconsciously she picked all of the colors for her house based on the border by Brunschwig and Fils, which makes such a beautiful impression in her front hall.

BUNNY WILLIAMS I love beautiful hand-blocked wallpaper, particularly in a bathroom or in a hall. I wouldn't upholster a hall because it is not practical, but it gives a bedroom a sense of quiet. So I tend to think of the space. Wallpaper I love in halls, bathrooms, or in kids' rooms.

CATHY KINCAID We use wallpaper everywhere—it's soft and two-dimensional. It really does help a lot. For example, in a small room, we like a trellis paper or a bamboo design. It gives you depth, particularly if you are in a tiny space and it's an inside room with no or very few windows. I love tiny little patterns just as a background. There is nothing more fun than taking striped paper and making it like the inside of a little tent. Running it on the ceiling and running borders around it. But you have to be careful that it's not too busy, which could drive you crazy.

SUZANNE RHEINSTEIN Our living room is painted in stripes and it's glaze painted, so that the translucent quality of it is marvelous. It's very pretty the way the light falls. The ceiling is painted in Benjamin Moore's Palladian Blue. I've also done gray-blue. Once I did a room and we took all of the colors out of this beautiful old Dhurrie rug. The walls were a pale mango color and the ceiling was pale blue. In the dining room, the walls were a toasty cocoa and the ceiling was pink—that already is giving you something that is not startling, but is beautiful. It's a beautiful background for what you want to put in it. Another thing to do is to make the ceiling really shiny.

SUSAN BARTLETT CRATER In the Paleys' apartment, there was boiserie paneling in the living room. My grandmother told me that she had thought the room should be painted taxi cab yellow, so she had it painted that color. I don't know if she took that color from one of the amazing paintings the Paleys owned, but she had no fear about using paint—a bright paint—and hanging a Gauguin on it.

BRIAN McCARTHY Those panels looked fabulous in yellow with all of those paintings; I think that books can be a great form of decoration. Books create a tapestry. It doesn't mean that they have to be beautiful books per se; they can be any books—it's how you arrange them with objects and photographs.

CATHY KINCAID I am a Nazi about color in paint—everybody teases me. Painters hate me because I don't like paint that is sprayed on. There is a new bad habit that painters have now of spraying surfaces. They are the last trade to come in and have to be out quickly, and know they can do it faster if they spray everything. It makes the paint look like Formica—it looks terrible. The painters should be in the house for a long enough time to do a good job. The paintwork is the first thing you see when you walk in and it sets the tone for the entire house. If the paint is not right, there is no thread; if there is no thread that is taken through the house with color, then it's jarring. It's like being in a show house—each room is another new idea. I think that psychologically our brains compute that and it makes you uncomfortable. A lot of times that is what's wrong with houses when people call us in. They have just chosen the wrong paint colors.

The first thing you should do is hire the best painter you can afford. It should be someone who can mix paint on site, because the same color is going to look different in every room. It absorbs light differently. You can't go to the store and pick a color from a paint chip. When you come up with a color you like, don't put it against a white wall—take it to the room and put it against the wall and look at it, but don't put it against white. Anything you put against a white background is going to look a lot darker and a lot brighter. You need to move the paint color around the room and look at it at different times of the day. Put it in there and live with it. Don't just go off and get a paint chip because you saw it in a magazine or it's the new color. Try some different things. Put it in a room and look at it at different times of the day; live with it for several days. Make sure you really like it. Maybe it's a color you take out of a fabric or maybe it's a color that you pick out of a painting or a rug, but I think it is also very important not to match. I think when you match colors exactly the room loses something—it becomes boring and cheap.

FLOORS

I love painted floors and faux wood-patterned stained floors—I love all of that.

MARIO BUATTA

LIBBY CAMERON I have worked on a few houses with difficult floor plans and peculiar room shapes. One of these houses was a charming farmhouse in Waccabuc, New York. Upon opening the front door, directly ahead was a staircase with a living room on either side. Originally, one of the living rooms must have been a kitchen, but the house had been added on to many times without much thought. I decided to paint the floors and asked Chuck Fisher to help me connect these two rooms. We ended up going with a faux wood-grained checkerboard with a border around the edge and stars between the squares. It sounds busy but it wasn't—the tones were quiet and soft.

A long hallway in a house on an island in Maine was another instance when painting the floors was the only solution. At one end of the house on the ground floor, there had been two bedrooms that we took out and made into a large living room, installing three pairs of French doors along opposite walls that both faced the water, looking east and west. A hallway had to be created to get to the new living room; it ran along the east side of the house, past a library and dining room and closets; the hall had alcoves and was wider in some places than in others. We painted the floor in a big diagonal pattern, with marbleized squares between bands of a creamy off-white, with small red squares at the intersection of the bands and a red border following the shape of the entire space. The field of the floor was painted to look like a multicolored veined Portugese Portas marble with reds, blues, and light-brown veining on a beige background.

There was a house that I worked on when I was at Parish-Hadley that all of the decorators in the office talked about. Years before, Mrs. Parish worked on a farmhouse that had a separate building with a great room and a big kitchen where the family spent most of their time. Sadly, it burned to the ground.

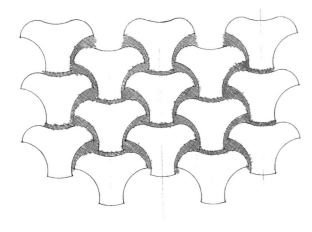

PAINTED FLOORS CAN ADD A WARMTH AND COHESIVENESS TO A ROOM. THIS FLOOR PATTERN WAS USED BY LIBBY CAMERON IN ONE OF HER PROJECTS.

These clients hired an architect who had done many institutional buildings at colleges and universities. Together they designed the addition that attached to the little farmhouse. Their design was very modern: you entered through a tower, which was probably eighteen or twenty feet high, that led into a hall. On the left was the old house and to the right was this new, modern structure. We all talked about how to marry the two spaces and to connect the textures and materials. The farmhouse had lovely old wide floorboards and the new wing had white oak floors. There were two steps, wide and curved, which led to the living room area, which had a curved window that was the length of the room, overlooking a meadow. There was an oval dining room behind the living room space. The kitchen was visible beyond the living room and shared the same views out over the property. There was a small seating area that backed up against a low wall that was meant to shield the kitchen. The living room was shallow, so the seating area was a bit awkward, and the seating area by the kitchen was small as well. The space was almost shaped like a parenthesis with a rectangle at the top and at the bottom of the curve. The challenge was to make sense out of a layout that really made no sense. We all talked about painting the floors, using a wallpaper as you came into the living room, to act as a bridge and a distraction between the old and the new. But there was no logical place to stop wallpaper, and given the shape of the living room, painting the floor in a classical way to support the integrity of the farmhouse just didn't work. It was a puzzle, and there really wasn't a good solution. In the end, we pickled the floors and glazed the walls, making the background as innocuous as possible, and let the patterns and materials create the warmth.

CATHY KINCAID We use enough sisal to wrap up the state of Rhode Island. It's great for those big houses that have floors going on forever. You put sisal down and it immediately gives a place a warmer, cozier feel. We use a lot of sisal under oriental rugs, because it can be hard to find an oriental that's the right size. It allows you more flexibility in your arrangement of furniture because you can have furniture that sits on and off of sisal. We use Wilton carpeting—a lot of the small patterns and some big patterns. I love the French linen carpets designed to look like old Dhurrie patterns. We use a lot of striped rugs, a lot of plain or cotton rugs. I try to avoid flowered or big patterns that are going to date, and stick to more geometric patterns. We use needlepoint rugs, though they are fragile.

Often I will have a Wilton carpet cut and bound so that it is almost the size of the room, leaving just a little bit of wood showing, instead of installing wall-to-wall carpeting.

JEFFREY BILHUBER I like all types of floors. There are certain factors to take into account for practicality. I do think that having a bare front hall is actually quite nice, unless you are trying to embrace the nineteenth-century town house, where it might be lovely to have a beautiful Wilton that's quiet. I have plenty of clients that like stone floors or painted wooden floors, or marquetry floors, and plenty of clients who just can't wait to put in wall-to-wall carpeting. Fine either way. Again, that is not really ever going to be the focus of the decorative resolution. It simply acts as a vehicle to deliver all the other messages. There are a lot of people who obsess over the floors. I think all the floors in my house are just painted. They have wonderful big planks that were never meant to be exposed. It's junk wood that they slapped on there because they basically let the prosperity materialize in terms of a great fireplace surround, or molding or casing. You see it historically, globally—you see it all the time. Grand houses have these very basic floors because they were technically meant to be covered, either by paint or furniture or carpet, and it's what surrounds you that is meant to be more seductive.

SISTER PARISH DESIGN'S "DOLLY" FABRIC IS USED IN THE TÊTE DE NEGRE
COLORWAY IN A LIBRARY DESIGNED BY CATHY KINCAID. THE HOUSE WAS BUILT IN
1746 AND IS USED AS A SUMMER RETREAT FOR A YOUNG DALLAS FAMILY.

FABRICS

If you think about how we at Colefax have worked with some of the same fabrics for years, yet every single room where they are used looks completely different. EMMA BURNS

LIBBY CAMERON I remember the sample room at Parish-Hadley and loving the wide variety of colors and textures of the sample fabrics, which were all beautifully arranged in neat stacks. It was intoxicating. There were two walls of fabric swatches stacked up to the ceiling, with rugs below. By seeing stacks of fabric like that, you begin to understand how many different tones of blues or reds there are—it is like being in a paint store, but so much more. That is an invaluable thing to learn, to notice and to understand, that there are so many subtle differences in colors, the yellow tints or green casts—there are thousands of variations in every color. As a child and still today, I can remember almost anyone's telephone number, and my mind works that same way with color. I can remember the shade of a yellow wall that I was in last year, or even years ago. Some colors make me feel so happy and energized that they stay in my head. I loved digging around in that sample room—it was exciting looking at all of those beautiful colors and patterns.

TODD ROMANO It is not like we are a regulated field. There are a lot of different ways to skin a cat. I always say this to clients: there are a million different ways you can approach a job. And I think that is a very interesting thing, to allow yourself to have the freedom of thought, to not be hindered by preconceived notions, but to come to it with a very free and open mind. I ask myself, "Does it lay out well on a sofa, or is it the right weight for curtains? Is it right for an upholstered sofa?" Those are the sorts of things that not everyone understands, because they haven't had that sort of training. I think that is what I took away from those eight and a half years of working at two different firms. If anybody came to me and asked, "Well, I want to get in to this business—

what should I do?" I would say go get a job with the very best firm you can, even if you are carrying coffee into the office and folding samples. One of my first jobs with Mario was cleaning up the sample room.

EMMA BURNS The thing we fight against the whole time is that sort of globalization. The magazines, which are of course fantastic in so many ways, have opened the floodgates in letting everybody into the secrets, and the decorators have to work even harder and turn tricks. We have a lot of things custom-made for each job. We will have things made in India, we'll have fabrics printed or whatever, just to try to achieve something that is really unique.

MARTHA ANGUS I love prints. I have always loved Fortuny—I never get tired of that. I also find that since my degree is in painting, I like to work with art collectors, so I consider the art to be the pattern and don't want the fabrics to compete with them.

EMMA BURNS I like woven fabrics, I like linens, I like textured things. I love mohair and things that are deep and lush. I was saying we have a lot of things specially woven; we work a lot with a mill in Florence that makes beautiful linens, which have such a lovely sort of dryness and look relaxed. When they are put on a chair they look sensational, because they are a wonderful balance. I suppose I like all of those old favorites like Fortuny and beautiful fabrics from Claremont, and I like to use funny things like a sari cut up as lampshades, so that you get a little bit of print to get a more interesting look. I often do that with stripes—I railroad them on upholstery, which can make things look a little younger, add a little twist.

CATHY KINCAID I used a silk velvet for two cushions in my living room, and my cat destroyed them. You just have to think about the appropriateness of fabrics. What's going to be comfortable to sit on? What's going to wear well?

SUSAN BARTLETT CRATER Many people think Sister loved floral chintzes more than any other fabrics, but that was not true at all. My favorite rooms are the ones in which she used it sparingly and mixed it with non-traditional Alan Campbell geometric prints, or fabrics she had collected from her travels in Africa and South America. Libby and I started our fabric and wallpaper collection almost ten years ago when we thought it was just too sad that all of the custom Parish-Hadley prints she loved would no longer be around. We resurrected many of those, as well as reproduced prints from the snippets and cuttings of fabric Sister had collected over the years. There is a large wooden cupboard in her house in Maine, which my mother owns now, where her fabric collection is stashed. She had collected a lot of it to use in the collages she made, or they were leftover yardage from furniture she had upholstered in a one-of-a-kind print she had picked up traveling. She loved quilts because she had grown up with them, as well as the simple cottons that were used in the summer houses in Maine. When she was working on a room she thought of the fabric first. In the first house she decorated, she used mattress ticking for curtain material. In describing the room she wrote, "I then had another inspiration and used white mattress ticking for the curtains. Mrs. Parish thought they were sheets and wondered why I hadn't left the windows bare until the curtains arrived. The whole room was reflected in large mirrors, enhancing our pleasure and Mrs. Parish's shock." I have often wondered if some of her earliest innovations were devised simply to shock her mother-in-law. It would not be surprising.

She also loved to use simple cotton chintz on important furniture to humanize it and make it more accessible in a grand room. She said that wonderful, interesting fabrics could compensate for a room that lacked architectural merit, and you can see this in many of her rooms, particularly in Maine.

The abundance of material in the linen closets in Maine also reflect the variety of fabrics she loved. The closets house her varied collections of tablecloths and napkins, a wide variety of colors, prints, linens, cottons, felts—all to set the table inside and out. Libby and I have used some of her favorites for our print collection.

LIBBY CAMERON Mrs. Parish knew what she liked and followed her instinct. She would know that she wanted to use a certain pattern, so I would have to fill it out with rugs and wallpaper and find furniture. I would start with the colors that were in the print and look for different weight fabrics and a variety of textures and smaller prints to work with it. Then Mrs. Parish would look at it. You know how she used to roll her eyes—like that? Well, I knew immediately if I'd gotten what she wanted. Albert's expressions weren't as much of a giveaway; he was also more explicit at the beginning about what direction he wanted to take.

MARIO BUATTA Today it's chintz—yesterday it was beige. I remember 1990—the end of the eighties—the period of everybody spending money and doing things and too much chintz. Peggy Kennedy said chintz is out, and the next month everything went beige. Albert was beige. Everything was beige, beige, and beige. All of a sudden in 2005 beige is out—it's finished, it's over. It's silly. You should live with what you are happy with. I have been happy in the same room with the same color for years. My room is pistachio green. Three or four shades of it, and it has been that way since 1976. I have never changed anything.

BRAIN McCARTHY When I look back at Mrs. Parish and her work, I think of several fabrics that she tended to use more than others. I remember working with her on Enid Haupt's apartment. When it was finished, basically that big drawing room had only two fabrics—one was "Floral Bouquet." To me that was brilliant—that she went in and created something that was so complex yet so simple at the same time. Within that one chintz pattern, she used all different parts of it to create different vignettes on the chairs, and it created this great eclectic combination—you wouldn't have realized that it was all from just one fabric.

CATHY KINCAID You have to take each situation case by case. There is nothing prettier than a room that is of all the same fabric—to use just one fabric even if it's a big print, a floral—on all the chairs, especially in a bedroom or a sun room. But if that is not the direction of the room, I think you really do need to use some solid colors and vary the textures. Maybe choose a fabric to use in the room somewhere, and take all of your colors out of that or take them out of the rug. I feel more comfortable with solid colors on the big pieces. Usually we use a linen velvet on a sofa because it's bulletproof. You have to think about the dirt factor because you want people to be able to enjoy their furniture. You don't want them to feel like they can't eat on it or lie down on it. We like to use a lot of old textiles, although it's not always practical to use them on pieces you sit on all the time. I think the old textiles add softness and richness and a quirkiness that you can't get from a new fabric.

SUZANNE TUCKER I am not of the school that more is more, but I am definitely not of the school that less is more. To me it's all about a refined balance of sheen and texture and how all of those things have to play together. That's one thing they need to teach more in design school—how to use fabrics to play off each other. It's not too dissimilar from dressing yourself. If you put on a brocade jacket and a brocade dress and brocade shoes and a brocade handbag—it's like *my god*. So it's about the balance and the contrast. There is this inundation in the market of chenilles. Well, you can only use one chenille in the room! Or if you use too many velvets in a room, nothing stands out and nothing shows up. To me texture is hugely important. For example, a lot of people love mohair—there are maybe three mohairs on the market that I would even consider using because, for me, they just feel horrible. They're itchy. I don't understand why you would want to sit on them. That's a big part of decorating, not just the visual, but the tactile, and when you sit in a chair how it envelops you, how it feels on your skin, how the arm feels in your hand. It's all about your senses and comfort.

MASTERING
the MIX

In every room it's good to have something a little bit off—humble elegance within a perfect room.   EMMA BURNS

LIBBY CAMERON I think that too many people think everything in a room has to match, that people are scared to combine glass and lacquer and wood. That was one of the most important things I learned while at Parish-Hadley, that in fact it is the combination of textures and surfaces that make a space work. Mrs. Parish was led by her instincts and Albert is more academic. So I got the best education imaginable, being able to learn by looking through both their eyes. It was quite clear in the beginning that they each took a different approach to a project. I learned very quickly what I needed to find for each of them in terms of types of fabric or trimmings, styles of furniture, and types of rug. But they both always mixed up their rooms with a medley of textures and scale. I learned that nothing was wrong with, or better than, using a variety of textures and different patterns. Albert liked the cleaner lines; Mrs. Parish liked the unexpected.

BRIAN McCARTHY To me it's paint, lacquer, gilded woods, any different variety of things—bronze, gilt bronze, whatever.

SUZANNE TUCKER The difficult thing now, and I tell the clients this, is that mistakes are expensive, more so than I think they ever were in the past. The world is more expensive, textiles are more expensive—all that sort of thing. Try things out for a while. Get a yard of fabric and lay it over the sofa and live with it

SISTER PARISH DESIGN'S "DESMOND" WALLPAPER AS WELL AS "ELIZA" AND "CAMPBELL" FABRICS ARE USED IN SISTER PARISH'S GRANDSON'S BEDROOM IN HER MAINE SUMMER HOUSE. A COLLECTION OF CHILDREN'S PORTRAITS COVER THE WALLS.

for a month. See what happens with the light in the room—see if you still love it after a month. That's something I advise people starting out.

TODD ROMANO A lot of people lose track of form, function, scale. All of these things take precedence long before we get into what color the room is going to be. I see a lot of people running around our building and what not, saying, "Oh what a pretty fabric," and I think, "It is a pretty fabric, but what are you going to do with it?"

LIBBY CAMERON I appreciate how Europeans live, especially the English. In their houses, there are beautiful pieces of older furniture mixed in with upholstery. Some of it looks like it is quite worn but it's being used, and no one is fretting about coasters or marring the wood of a table. They mix it all up and the scale is different—it's all much gutsier furniture. They have an understanding of how to use what they have, which this country doesn't have. The English know how to live, and are not scared to mix different periods, or use lacquer furniture with painted furniture or with tattered upholstery. I find that everyone in this country is far more cautious and timid.

PETER DUNHAM David Hicks's front hall was very kind of grand in a way. It had a stone floor and a very pretty, big Georgian architectural fireplace, and there might have been a very big rocking horse. It was very architectural with very big crown molding and a wonderful floor. It was very much about the architecture. The house itself in many ways was quite simple. The living room had this very pretty fabric—it was a woven beige and cream on the upholstered walls above the baseboard. He had a mixture of English upholstery and French painted furniture. There was a white-painted console with all his stuff on top and a mixture of contemporary art and family things. There were so many different rooms, that were all so interesting. There was this beautiful little octagonal room that he had made rather Gothic, which he loved. He put in this early nineteenth-century Gothic fireplace. Everywhere there were interesting things—your eye was constantly drawn to something. For example, he would

SISTER PARISH'S SUMMER HOUSE LIVING ROOM FURNITURE WAS
REUPHOLSTERED IN "CLARA" AND "BURMESE" FROM THE SISTER PARISH
DESIGN FABRIC COLLECTION.

have covered a chair in a beautiful fabric, and he would say the Queen of Togo gave that material to me. It was all kind of gutsy and yet rather casual in a very fancy way. He adored those big tables with structured rows of vodka and Coca-Cola—the bottles all perfectly laid out. Everywhere you went there were things to notice.

MILES REDD I think about how to use old textiles versus new textiles—something that is silk velvet versus something that is linen versus something

Mita Corsini Bland

that is from Urban Outfitters versus something from Clarence House. For me it's all about the mix of high/low silk, nubby raw satin that makes a room interesting—I guess it's all of those things that go into creating that balance that people are after. Although I think everyone does want the "wow"—the glamour—at the same time, you don't want it to be so intense that you are sitting at the edge of your chair, completely uncomfortable.

I would not say I am the most textile-driven person. I am more about color and flow and objects. There are one hundred different reds out there, different blues, different whites, so it's really okay if we have something grand here—let's have something cozy there. If we have something cozy, let's have something grand beside it. It's just that mixture of back and forth. It is instinctual. I can't always articulate it—you just see it.

EMMA BURNS There is a sort of perfection in imperfection. Like something that is slightly cracked, or something like that, so that you cut the level and bring the proper balance to things, because if everything is museum quality or everything is very poor, it doesn't work. You need that balance. It is like a recipe.

JOSIE McCARTHY I always do the rug last. That is the opposite of most people. Unless, of course, it is a major rug. I just did a town house in New York, and in the drawing room we started with the rug because it was an important one. Usually, I work with the colors and the fabrics and from there the rugs. I am doing a modern town house now and it is the fourth house I have done for these clients over twenty-something years. We recovered the sofas that they bought from me twenty years ago. They were great sofas. They are very modern and very geometrical but they kind of warm it up.

SUZANNE TUCKER I'll tell you an interesting story. I was working on a historic house in Belvedere, California, for about five years. These clients

BRUNSCHWIG & FILS'S "SAVONS ET SENTEURS" WALLPAPER ADDS WARMTH AND CHARM TO THIS BATHROOM.

had multiple houses all around the world, including Singapore, Australia, and Vancouver. She brought in a feng shui master from China to look at the plans and to help lay out how things should be placed in the house. The master bedroom was a challenging space with extraordinary views of the Golden Gate Bridge. The feng shui master put the bed right in front of the window. You walked in, looked down the length of the room, and the bed faced you in the doorway, which is what feng shui is all about. How do you argue with a feng shui master who was flown in from China? I tried to talk her out of it and suggested she put the bed against the wall but she was adamant. So I created a canopy bed with sheer curtains behind the bed. Even though there was light from the window coming in, it was filtered. You're not meant to walk in on the bed. Feng shui is actually based on ancient Chinese warrior tactics. It's all about protection. It's all about placing yourself so you can see your enemies coming at you. The desk in an office should face the door so that you see people coming toward you; you don't want to have your back to the door. It's subtle common sense anyway. Where do you feel better? Do you feel better having your desk facing this way or that way?

LIBBY CAMERON Nothing can ever really be perfect, but it can feel perfect. I'm always amazed by combinations of colors and textures and furniture, and how mixing things up makes a room more interesting and adds character. I like it when things are slightly off—it feels more real. There are so many ways to approach any space, and everyone will have a different opinion, but it all really comes back to common sense and needs: the hearth, the center, the requirements people have, and then how what you use fulfills those needs.

COLLECTIONS

Sister told me that every house should have a collection. Her early memories of antiquing with her father were important to her. She didn't care about the value or how these collections were garnered or even how old or new they were. What she cared about was the love and attention they represented for the family that collected them. Her most oft-repeated quote was, "Tradition is the lucky part of my life," and she really meant it. She had an ivory collection on her desk in New York; and wicker, porcelain, and folk art collections in Maine; and she made sure her grandchildren were launched with collections she thought suited them. Somehow she got it in her head that my brother Harry liked birds, so he got bird prints from my grandfather, his namesake, at Christmas. I am not sure how that rumor started, and to this day I don't think he even thinks about birds, but Harry ended up with some nice prints. My mother has always been given apples because her nickname is Apple and so on. She liked the idea of houses as places of history. In describing the Summer House in Maine she said, "There is not a thing in this house that doesn't have a complete story of our life together" (referring to my grandfather). I know that the hodgepodge of inexpensive prints and paintings my husband and I have bought over the years in Europe are among our favorite possessions because of the memories they hold of those trips.

—SUSAN BARTLETT CRATER

Expressing personal feelings and memories is the essence of decorating. I find that people who can abandon the old screen porch, hide the wicker without paint, or uproot the first rosebush they ever planted are lacking in feelings for what I call "home." Hundreds of roses can't make up for the pride you felt in that first bush. That is true of your first room, your house, your first possession.

—SISTER PARISH

A CREAMWARE COLLECTION IS BEAUTIFULLY SET OFF IN A CABINET IN TODD ROMANO'S LIVING ROOM.

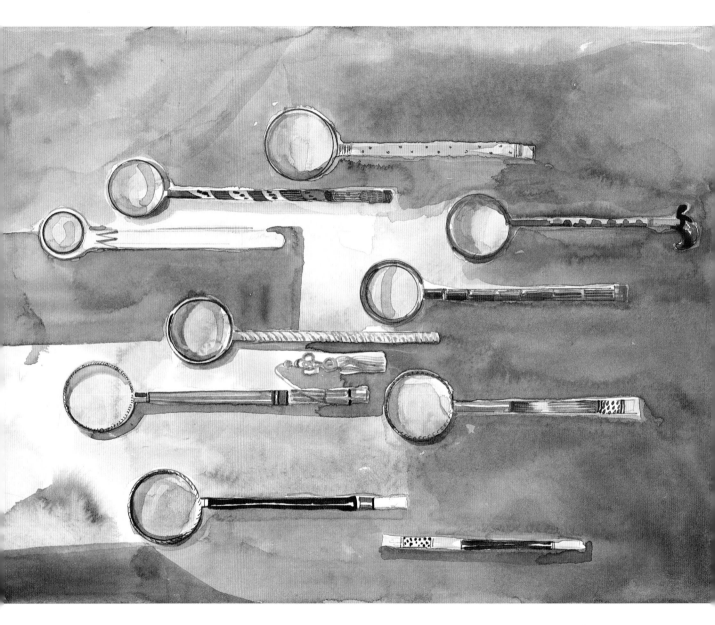

A COLLECTION OF ANTIQUE MAGNIFYING GLASSES.

STARTING a COLLECTION

An art dealer friend of mine told me that he thought that the best art collections were created when people kept the paintings they bought when they had no money. He thought it important that they are still in the collection and also the idea of keeping the mistakes. Because when everything has been so refined and upgraded the collection starts to lose its personality.

DANIEL ROMUALDEZ

JANE CHURCHILL In England we are blessed in having houses that were handed down from generation to generation. A lot of families have added collections to them. Different collections of different things. Like the Cholmonoleys collected amazing soldiers. They have got these incredible collections of soldiers and battles. The Butes were amazing—every single generation collected something from tartan boxes to pictures, furniture, etc. There are certain clients for whom we have done very good collections of furniture, but this was always done with somebody to advise us, because although I know what I like, I certainly don't have the knowledge to tell what is real and what isn't. I think a lot of decorators have gotten themselves in trouble by buying whatever, and then it turns out to be made up. It is really important to use an adviser. You learn, the client learns, everybody learns—rather than reading a piece of paper that says it's French. The fact is you just learn much more about the furniture. You learn more, you get a better eye, and I think that is important. With respect to how to display collections, I think it's nicer when they are not lined up. I think it's nicer when they are more involved in what is in the house.

ALBERT HADLEY Brooke's library with her collection of Vincent's books was one of my favorite rooms, because it was for her really—and this was the way it all came about. The idea was that we bring out and shelve her husband's old library—books that had been in storage since his death, and that was the whole point. Brooke called and asked me to come to tea, and I thought, what's up now? I got there and she was very nervous because Jeffrey Bennison, the decorator from London, was in town and she didn't want Sis to know it. Brooke knew Sis was going to be very angry because she was going to have Jeffrey redo the room that Sis had just done. I held my tongue as much as I could but I said, "Brooke, it's your house. You can have anybody you want. You don't have to worry about Sis. She will be disappointed, but we both know Jeffrey and he is a great guy." Since Vincent had died I had heard nothing about Vincent's library—it was all in storage. At that point the library just had the brown chintz and the room was sort of no color. It was a fake room. It was built with the building. I said, "But what is he going to do?" and she said, "Oh I will show you—it's wonderful fabric." She came back with the fabric and I agreed it was wonderful fabric. Without even thinking what I was saying, I said to her, "You know, Brooke, fabric doesn't necessarily make a room." "Are you telling me something?" she asked. I said, "Well, there is nothing fake in your life except this room and I think if I were going to redo the room I would take a different approach." "Really, what do you mean?" I had no idea what I was talking about but it was a good line and—it was true. I said, "You have all of Vincent's books and I would…" Anyway I went on with the conversation about what to do. I said I think it should be classic, but they always want to know the color even before where the door goes. I said I think it should be red and I pointed to something in a painting. Oh, she got very excited, so I went back and did a sketch. It went around and finally we did the room. Well, Sis was furious. Obviously very jealous. Every week I would get a report of how unhappy Brooke was because it was taking so long. Of course I would see Brooke, and she was having the time of her life. She was loving it. So why shouldn't that be my favorite project? She loved it.

WILLIAM HODGINS I started collecting creamware when I was at the Parish office, when you could buy a plate for $1.50. Of course, that was forty years ago. Nobody cared very much about creamware so I was able to buy a few pieces. That's how I started. It seems now that I am collecting rather unusual chairs. Do you remember Gene Tyson? He died a few years ago. I am his executor and Gene left me a wonderful, peculiar Italian chair—gilt and the nailhead trim is wood. I realized when I put it in my living room that I have five kinds of unusual, peculiar, handsome chairs and I have four more somewhere else. Maybe that's my little collection although I never meant it to be one. I don't really like seeing collections on tables where they are just going to get in the way.

TOM SCHEERER I'm not one for collections. I always prefer a succinct and dynamic arrangement of disparate rather than like objects when making a tablescape or arranging a wall of pictures. But I do love anything brown! I'm drawn to natural, beige, and brown in the way that I never am to blacks and grays.

In my New York apartment I have a brown and white Lee Krasner gouache above a brown and sepia Ben Nicholson lithograph above a brown table with a shiny brown *coco de mer*, several burnished natural bamboo and brown ceramic *objets de vertu*. The walls are white so it all works.

CATHY KINCAID You educate yourself by talking to people when you buy something. Buying at auction is educational. I think just looking at furniture, porcelain, or antique fabrics is how you learn. If you look at a lot of it you start to be able to separate the good from the not so good. I do tell my clients to buy only what they like and what they can afford. If you look at a blue and white porcelain plate and you're not sure when it was made, obviously, you can't know what it is worth. If you look at it and you're not sure, but it's a price that you can afford, it's beautiful to you, and it works in the space—buy it. But don't go spending three times what you can afford because you think it's what you should have. It's going to look the same as something that costs much less. Maybe it's not as fine, but who cares unless you are a real collector, unless you are an investment collector. Even those people get fooled sometimes. My

second job was in Dallas with a man called John Astin Perkins, and he was one of the three first big designers there. He had an architecture degree and he was from a very wealthy family himself. So one day he got a shipment of antique porcelain, which he had recently bought in France. He brought the porcelain in and he told me it was supposedly one hundred years old. He said, "Cathy, clean this one base up, we'll just get the dirt off it, and we'll make it into a lamp." So when I cleaned it up—and this is someone who bought all the time—we realized that he had paid way too much for it and it was not what he thought it was. Even someone who was an expert was fooled.

BRIAN McCARTHY I used to go to the flea markets and pick up interesting paintings and things, really stylish stuff that I still have. I have a great pair of paintings that were by some guy who was a principal dancer in the New York City Ballet in the late 1940s. He did cubist paintings. His passion was as an artist and they are really good. I paid $400 for the pair of them and I took them to Heydenryk and they put great frames on them. You know what—they look like really good paintings. So there are lots of ways of tricking the eye. What people need to realize is you have to spend enough time looking at things so you can begin to discern what's unusual and what's not. That's what makes a collection. You develop it and, bit by bit, make it more interesting. Not to say you have to spend a year looking before you start buying, but as you get into the process you begin looking, looking, looking. If it's a fun thing to do, you are naturally going to evolve into collecting things that you might not have expected to collect.

I think your eye becomes educated. If you are curious, you are going to educate yourself.

MITCHELL OWENS To me collections aren't about quality or provenance. Anybody with pots of money and a savvy adviser can pull off an important assemblage. I'm more often drawn to collections with a soul and a story, which may not represent a major investment, but which add a huge dose of personality to a room.

A friend of mine, Jacqueline Coumans, an interior decorator in New York City, collects milk glass. Pale blue in her country house and white in her city apartment. The pieces are very inexpensive, generally speaking, with covered dishes shaped like hens sitting on their nests or toothpick holders in the form of owls or great footed bowls. She has tons of it, thanks to a young son who bought her a piece of milk glass, thinking, in a naïve child's way, that it was like the Sèvres porcelain they had inherited. Jacqueline was so charmed, and so anxious not to disappoint her son with the truth, that she just let him use his allowance to buy pressed milk glass for her! Twenty-odd years later, all her friends do, including me. I can't go to a flea market or eBay without picking up a piece for her. She masses it all together to marvelous decorative effect in cabinets or on tabletops, so something cheap becomes something impressive, even stately. And it is a collection she actually uses. The milk-glass plates go from display to dinner table, the milk-glass goblets are handed around at parties, etc. Collections don't have to be precious to be important. And if they are objects one actually uses and handles on a daily basis, the collection becomes essential rather than merely admired.

In England I once visited the home of the designer Oriel Harwood and her then husband, the writer Stephen Calloway. The stairwell of their Georgian house in the Camberwell section of London was loaded with busts, mounted on brackets, tucked on a windowsill, perched on steps. It was the most fantastically impressive and rather alarming display, ranging from marble busts of obscure classical worthies to a massive fiberglass head. The effect was like a Piranesi etching of ancient Rome come to life, though the couple had been inspired by Sir John Soane. Again, it was all about the grand gesture, not the quality of the elements.

When I lived in Morocco I started collecting souvenir pictures depicting the great Qaaba in Mecca, that impassive block of black stone. The pictures are truly souvenirs, large colorful pieces of silk, pink or black or gold or green, all embroidered or spangled with glitter. They are what a devout Muslim would buy to prove that one had made the pilgrimage to Mecca. I only managed to find a half dozen or so in the flea market, Bab Khmis, in Marrakech, over two years, though I hope to remedy that in the future. They really are quirky and unusual.

I would love to have a collection of needlework pictures and hang them all over a small cozy room. Scenes of gardens and images of courtiers, everything from humble country cross-stitchery to a fabulous example of Jacobean stump work. I only have a few indifferent twentieth-century needlework pictures at the moment, but I keep my eyes peeled.

LIBBY CAMERON I have been collecting animals for years. I went to boarding school outside of Boston and one day when I was out and about with a bunch of friends, I spotted a wonderful old sign on a barn. I was able to get it from the owner, it was in terrible condition, but it had a wonderful painting of a cow and had "Jerseys" painted above. I took it back to my room, cleaned it up, and restored it as best I knew how with Q-tips, soap, and water, and to this day it hangs in my house. That started my collection, and over the years I have amassed quite a few different types of collections, all having to do with animals. There are about forty very small watercolors in our library that I have been buying over the years from a dealer in Vermont. There is a large wooden cow that I got from John Rosselli, which lives on the ledge of the bay window in our living room, and a trio of porcelain cats on a nearby table watching him. There are English porcelain roosting hens and some odd chickens on the mantel. There is a huge Indian elephant in the dining room, painted on linen, which takes up an entire wall, across from a beautiful collection of blue-and-white Chinese export that I inherited not long ago. I like to mix it all up and in together. The house is small and the collections seem to keep growing, so they all meld into one another and are compatible.

BUNNY WILLIAMS A collector is a very serious person. I'm really a purchaser. I buy things that I love. A collector will wait five years to find the one plate that they don't have in their collection. That's not me. For example, if I see a bronze sunflower, I am going to love something like that, because I love my garden and I love nature. I tend to buy objects that can be dog-related, garden-related, but I am not a serious collector. I am not an academic collector.

MARTHA ANGUS I usually try to get my clients into art if they aren't—if they express any interest at all. I have one client right now and I took him to Art Basel Miami last year, which I go to every year. That's my favorite event in the whole wide world. We went to the satellite fairs and to the main convention. Have you ever been there? It's the most intense thing. It's essentially every major art gallery in the world all in one place. It's pretty fabulous. So we did a lot of shopping there and he is very smart—a bright Silicon Valley client. They remind me of my old Wall Street clients, as they may not know a lot about art, but they are so great because they want to learn, and really, you can teach them pretty quickly. A lot of times I'll lend my clients stacks and stacks of auction catalogues. You can read them in bed, and if the clients are a husband and wife, I say you tag the ones you each like and let's just see where you're at. Sometimes I even take them to the museums.

ALBERT HADLEY Obviously, when Bill Paley bought a Picasso, he knew what he was buying, but he bought a picture because he liked the picture. He liked the subject. It wasn't bought for a specific room.

MITCHELL OWENS The other thing I keep in mind is that if a particular style or period is hot, it's good to steer clear of it and try to find a period that is undervalued. Right now, brown furniture of numerous periods is considered not sexy and so is going for relatively bargain prices. The market for eighteenth-century American and English furniture, excepting the finest of the fine, is also flat. French Provincial, American Empire, aka pillar-and-scroll—same thing. I am crazy about American Empire, but so few people are, even though one can acquire quite good and very decorative pieces for very little financial outlay. The period is considered too bulky and too dark, but to me American Empire furniture is quite often wonderfully unadorned and has powerful silhouettes.

JEFFREY BILHUBER I can't put soul into a house. It is the responsibility of the client. When you look at great nineteenth-century decorators and early twentieth-century decorators, the idea of a fully developed and formed house being delivered in its entirety was foreign to them. It is a relatively new phenomenon where houses are delivered 100 percent complete. Don't get me wrong—I adore it because I love the entire process of seeing a house with fires lit and food in the fridge and children jumping up and down on the sofa. That's wonderful for me to see. So if we can speed that process up it's brilliant. Invariably great architects and decorators of the nineteenth and early twentieth centuries were responsible for delivering a beautiful shell. They would get the basic furniture in the room. They would get the basic volume of the curtains on the window. But the personality and the decorative accessories and the nuances were the responsibility usually of the mistress of the house or the owner. They didn't provide books or objects on the table or libraries or paintings. The great decorator provided a stage and we still do.

DISPLAY

Collections will be lifeless if you have little things and you spread them out too thinly. They have much more strength when they are used all together and arranged well. LIBBY CAMERON

TOM SCHEERER I designed a game room for a large house in Hobe Sound, Florida, using a collection of reproduction bird prints. The house sits on the Jupiter Island Club golf course, which borders the Intracoastal Waterway. It's interesting that the founders and a lot of members of the Jupiter Island Club are longtime conservationists and avid bird watchers, so the course really is a fascinating bird sanctuary for migratory and indigenous species. My client spends hours watching, feeding, and tending to the bird life at her doorstep: swans, owls, heron, egrets. So the "ornithological" is very much part of the house's story and the story of the client who grew up in this very room.

The prints are superb reproductions, from a complete eighteenth-century portfolio by Olaf Rudbeck, a Swedish naturalist. The prints were brought to the United States by Merrill Stenbeck, the late antiquary (Valley House Antiques), and my dear friend Merrill was instrumental in my being hired by this Hobe Sound client. The room is soaring, at least twenty feet tall, so we framed the whole portfolio with no fear it could not be accommodated in its entirety. So in several ways, the prints are an apt decoration for this room.

I initially laid the main block of prints, which are over the sofa, out on the floor. I wanted a strong and interesting graphic quality to the interlocking sizes and shapes of the frames. Additionally, with the juxtaposition of the sinuous shapes of the birds, we created a wonderful dynamic "calligraphic" effect. The balance of the prints are sprinkled around the room in apt locations: an owl peering down from the barnlike ceiling, sandpipers scurrying along a long tabletop. The rest of the room was designed with the prints in mind. I chose muted fabrics and an earthy carpet to allow the birds to "fly," to be the dominant design motif in the room.

This game room has a large flat-screen television and card table, and is the most decidedly masculine of the house's several living rooms, loggias, etc. The love of wildlife is a common ground between the men and the women of this family!

LIBBY CAMERON Something very few people know how to do well is arrange collections and hang art. My Uncle Rory was famous for his tablescapes, for knowing how to arrange objects and collections on tables as well as walls. It's a process of adding and subtracting, of editing. Some things people collect are just not very interesting because they are too much the same. Whereas if you have a really interesting mix of boxes, for instance, and they are all different textures, lacquer along with tortoiseshell, it's much more interesting. A lot of people don't understand that. It goes back to the whole premise of brown wood. People feel very safe if everything in a room is brown and wooden or of the same period or style. It's safe, but it kills a room and takes all the energy out of it. Also people get very locked into collections and how they were displayed when they inherited them. For instance, if you have some hideous piece of furniture that was in a hallway at your grandmother's house, it doesn't have to go in your hallway. Often a coat of paint on it can be great and it might fit well in the bathroom.

BRIAN McCARTHY It's what we learned from Albert. I think the one thing that I would credit Albert with forever, for all time, is what a great eye he has for editing. It's like a painter knowing when to stop; it's a process of adding and subtracting. You know—you put four things on a table and if it looks crowded you take one away. If the balance doesn't look right put it back in and take another piece away. It's all about trial and error.

When people start collecting things, it's not about having instant collections. Part of the fun of doing it is that it takes a long time. For instance, when I started

A MAGNIFICENT COLLECTION OF REPRODUCTION BIRD PRINTS DOMINATES A GAME ROOM DESIGNED BY TOM SCHEERER.

collecting black-and-white photography years ago, I didn't even start hanging things probably for two years. I needed to get enough so I could start to create a composition with it. Over time you begin to move things around, and for me it segued into colored photography and more contemporary things.

At Parish-Hadley we would only accessorize because in those days a lot of clients already had things. Whereas now I find very often there is less stuff that a client comes to you with and they are generally more interested in starting, I don't want to say from scratch, but with less. I try to get clients out, to begin to get their eyes seeing things. I watch what they react to even before we begin shopping. I say, let's go to ten stores—ten antiques dealers—and you tell me what you find interesting and I will point out to you what I find appropriate given what we have been talking about.

Everything in my apartment is like a scrapbook. I remember where everything came from, which is fun. Some things make the cut and some things don't. Some things move out of your life and some things move to another part of your life. As you redecorate over the years suddenly you look around and say, wow, I've got a really good collection of portraits. So you really make a point with something like that, which can make a very strong visual impact. Plus, learning to step outside one's parents' shoes—that's another thing that I sometimes hear—my parents did this and my parents did that. It's like, *oh my god*!

PETER DUNHAM I like to create impact. When I'm in the room it's actually quite simple. It's all kind of simple and it layers up. The layer is different for every person. You might want to layer the one Rothko and another person might want to layer the twenty-seven dog paintings.

SUSAN BARTLETT CRATER A collection is demeaned if it is displayed awkwardly or with pretention. It should gain strength from its display. Brooke Astor had an amazing collection of dog paintings and they were hung going up a very grand staircase in her house in the country. The mixture of big and small paintings added to the interest of the paintings. Nothing is worse than the little diddly collections of silver or small boxes scattered all over the tables in a living room. There can be strength in numbers. It makes sense to group things together, as long as they don't look forced or like a stage set. My son Tucker's room in Maine had a portrait of my great-uncle as boy in it, and somehow a lot of other portraits of cousins, siblings, etc., ended up in that room—probably because there was no other place for them and they had sentimental value. If these portraits were hung individually you would say, who is that funny child, but together they represent many different styles of portraits of children. They are also enhanced by the offhand way they are hung, in a fairly casual, colorful room.

A SMALL COLLECTION OF ANTIQUE BALLS CREATES AN INTERESTING VIGNETTE ON A SITTING ROOM COFFEE TABLE.

BUNNY WILLIAMS It's funny sometimes when I go to work for somebody who wants to redo their house—one of the first things you find is that the house looks junky because all these little things have been stuck together with no relationship. One of the best things to do is to take everything out of the house and assemble it someplace else. I think it is fun to assemble like things. For example, everything that is white or blue or boxes or whatever. We try to look at all of the things people have and make some kind of sense out of them,

Mita Corsini Bland
06

so that when it is all put back it makes sense—instead of it just being a lot of stuff scattered all over the place. It's that whole thing—how do you arrange things? Obviously, we have a lot of dog things, so I have one table that has a collection of some marble dogs, a bronze dog, and a china dog. Instead of having them all over I did a collection of antique dog things. This makes it look interesting and makes more of a statement.

PETER DUNHAM I think what we add is never as strong as a great landscape or great art. I think what we do should be secondary to that, but I also think it's nice to defuse the seriousness of collections by making the decor a little bit more whimsical or a bit more like you collected this art from your granny's house.

SUSAN BARTLETT CRATER Albert Hadley will tell you that he doesn't like collections. I think that's because he just doesn't like the word. He is a natural collector and is always on the lookout for new and interesting artists or stylish objects. His sitting room in his apartment in New York has one of the most amazing collections of watercolor paintings you will ever see, from Van Day Truexes to unknown artists whose works have caught his eye. Books are everywhere in his houses and seem to be part of the landscape wherever you look. He once described his apartment as "a serene chiaroscuro tapestry woven with a bit of madness."

ALBERT HADLEY I try to avoid collections. I don't think it is necessary to think of collections as far as your living quarters are concerned. If you are a natural collector you will find a place to put them. Keep them together, don't scatter them all over the place. My mother bought all kinds of little trinkets but she had a thing about collecting glass slippers—she had dozens of them. There is something about the shape of a glass slipper, whether it is colored glass or china or painted or

A CHARMING COLLECTION OF SHELLS IS DISPLAYED IN NINA GRISCOM'S SHOP IN NEW YORK.

whatever. Some of them were on a shelf in her kitchen and some were somewhere else, but when you saw them it was like looking at a painting.

DANIEL ROMUALDEZ I try to incorporate collections from the beginning unless it's something awful and then you say, "Why don't you put it in the country?" The generating principle of the whole scheme typically involves whether they have a great picture collection or they collect sculpture or fabrics. For example, I have this client who inherited a lot of beautiful great master paintings from her father. We were renovating the apartment and I said, we don't need to spend a cent on redoing the moldings or the doors, we don't have to strip the walls, as your eye is only going to go to those beautiful paintings. So we spent the money on the kitchen. With someone who doesn't collect art, you have to do a lot more decorating, more color, more trims. I find that is also fun. The challenge is someone who has modern art. What's starting to happen is there are so many people who are collecting modern art, their apartments are starting to look alike. Everyone matches the decor to the painting so this is a challenge.

OUTDOOR ROOMS

SISTER PARISH'S PORCH IN MAINE HAS A WONDERFUL COLLECTION OF WICKER
FURNITURE, IRON TABLES, AND PLANT STANDS. THE ARCHED LATTICEWORK
ADDS AN ARCHITECTURAL ELEMENT TO THE PORCH AND FRAMES THE VIEW.

I grew up on the two most wonderful porches. My summers were spent in a cottage that teeters on the edge of a rock precipice in Maine. The house is called a "cottage"—it's a summer house with only fireplaces to keep you warm. My grandparents found and loved this house, and filled it all summer long with family and friends, a Japanese cook, and a French governess for my father and my aunt. The house is filled with painted furniture, straw rugs, and lamps made from big colored glass jugs. There is nothing fancy about the house but it is comfortable, welcoming, and has the most beautiful views. There are two porches on the house, right next to each other, both overlooking the water and the islands—Damariscove, Squirrel Island, Fisherman's Island, White Island, and the sea beyond. One porch is screened in, the other one is open and has a rail around it to keep you from falling onto the rocks. There is an eclectic mixture of furniture on these porches, and over the years, many of the wicker pieces have fallen apart. It is so wonderful to sit there and just listen to the water hitting the rocks, to the sound of the bell buoys, to the cries of the seagulls, and, when the weather is bad, to the foghorn at Cuckle's Lighthouse.

Morning arrives each day with the sputtering noise of the engines of lobstermen's boats, the clanking of the winches that haul up the traps, and the smell of the water. We have breakfast on the screened-in porch, which faces due east. The sunlight shines across the water in a ribbony path, glistening and sparkling with the movement of the water. At times, depending on how clear the day is, it is very difficult to see across the water as the sun can be blinding.

My father always sat at the north end of the table. He was up before anyone else. The table was long and had wicker chairs around it—I don't remember that there were many chairs on the water side of the table. He began each morning by asking, "What are your plans for the day?" He always wants to have an activity planned, an agenda for the day—a sail or an excursion to one of the many islands, or a project like mending the screens on the porch that the dogs had broken through. It was hard to see him over the glare of the water even though he sat beside me.

In addition to the table on this screened-in porch, there were four rocking chairs with navy blue canvas seat and back cushions, with white buttons and piping. This was the porch used more during the day, as you were in the shade, and those rocking chairs were so comfortable. As a child, I loved to rock back and forth, with my feet on the horizontal rail that connects the screens, and read. The table became my project table. It was a wonderful place to paint rocks, make pictures out of abandoned periwinkle shells, draw, and do puzzles. It was very quiet and peaceful on that porch. The light is so wonderful at the end of the day when the sun is going down; the reflection on the sails of the boats going by casts the most wonderful glow of pinks, yellows, corals, and blues you can imagine. I have always loved watching the colors change as the sun goes down.

The open porch is wonderful, filled with pots of geraniums, petunias, ivy, and Queen Anne's lace. There are two seating areas, each with its back to the living room looking toward the sea. Years ago, there was a bench along the rail on two sides, with blue pillows to cushion your back; but the bench collapsed and was taken away. The painted wooden furniture disappears on this porch; you are only aware of the craggy rocks, the sound of the water, and the smell of the pines. It is a wonderful place to be when the breeze has died down at the end of the day, a lovely spot to sit until the mosquitoes come. Occasionally, a seagull will land on the rail to see if there are any stray crackers, only to take flight with a dramatic whooshing of wings. When standing, you look straight down onto the rocks fifteen feet below. There are sticks and logs, drying seaweed, and an occasional buoy from a lobster pot that has come loose and washed ashore. I always have a wonderful sensation of being suspended over the water when I sit there on what feels like a platform or a tree house, suspended between the house and the sea.

—LIBBY CAMERON

PORCHES and the GARDEN

In summer I think of porches: the nostalgic, varied, old-fashioned, enormously comfortable, and sometimes terribly stylish porches of American houses, outfitted for a long, hot season.

MARK HAMPTON, *Mark Hampton on Decorating*

SUSAN BARTLETT CRATER The Summer House porch in Maine is the center of the house. My grandmother loved her gardens and the view of the water more than anything else so she designed it that way. It is where we gather for all of the meals we can and always at the end of the day for a drink, weather permitting. Because there are no mosquitoes on the island, it is an open porch. It looks out on a lawn that slopes down to the ocean, which is really a little sheltered cove. Two long wooden docks in the distance and towering pine trees frame the little cove. From the porch there is a head-on view of Seven Hundred Acre Island, which is dominated by a large shingle-style house with multiple gambrel roofs. Nancy Lancaster was a frequent visitor to that house as it was owned by her sister, Mrs. Charles Dana Gibson. There are a pair of old green Adirondack chairs at the top of the steps leading down to the rocky beach and a dark green gazebo for changing into your bathing suit. Flower gardens border the lawn on either side.

The porch itself is set up a bit like a long living room. One end is covered and has a green canvas awning that can be extended if more shade is required on very hot days. Opposite the covered end is a lattice structure with two arched openings that frame the view. Sister had it installed to give the porch some architectural detail. Under the covered part there are two old wicker chaise longues that are upholstered with dark green canvas pillows with white piping. Ancient pillows with green leaf chintz are carelessly thrown on them as well. Small children and even teenagers like to sleep on the chaise longues on hot

nights. There is a long sideboard my grandmother would use as a buffet for meals. If it is not set up for meals, two large antique white glass swans hold pots of wild bay leaves in them. Next to this shady area, but out in the open, is a round table for meals that is covered by a faded yellow Mexican-looking umbrella with a little bell fringe. A couple of other seating areas are arranged on the remainder of the porch.

When visitors come to the house they walk from the gravel driveway, over a little bridge, and around the front of the house to the side where the porch sits. In this way they don't fully see the ocean until they turn the corner. This funny roundabout entrance gives whoever is sitting on the porch a full view of the newcomers approaching the house from the lawn. Three bedrooms can also be accessed directly from the porch so there is a constant feel of coming and going and that the action of the house takes place there.

The porch is currently arranged in almost the same manner as when my grandmother had it. It has the classic American porch color scheme of a gray wooden floor, light blue ceiling in the covered area, upholstered wicker painted a dark bottle green (which is two parts Benjamin Moore Essex Green and one part black mixed together), and masses of geraniums in clay pots or on antique metal shelves. In addition to this classic porch scheme, my mother has added her odd folk art chickens, old bird houses, and two funny-looking wooden rocking horses for her grandchildren. There are usually an array of wet bathing suits and brightly colored towels thrown over the railings. As porches are uniquely American, it makes sense to keep their decoration as such. Little is needed besides a good set of wicker furniture and a multitude of flowering plants. This porch is simple with little pretention as the view, the gardens, and the flowers on the porch tell the story.

MARIO BUATTA I have a Gothic country house with a porch that wraps around the entire house. It takes three hours to get there, though—it's a horrible ride. I open it and I close it. I haven't slept there since 1999. It's a long trip. You drive three hours and then you have to drive six miles to get a newspaper and container of milk. I love the house but the porch is falling off.

MARTHA ANGUS It's so true—porches are really important. I know they are important in the Hamptons, but they are even more important here in California. You really can use them, especially in San Francisco, where you can be outside almost every day of the year except for when it's raining. Native Californians say you just buy the same thing and you wear it all year. I thought, "Sure you do, that's the biggest line I've ever heard," but you do. It's more or less sixty to seventy the whole year, so you can be outside all the time.

Some of our clients have outdoor wood-burning fireplaces, which are fantastic. You really treat the outside just like a bona fide living room: it has an area carpet and comfortable furniture with lots of pillows, even upholstery; you are treating it like another room. You wouldn't put the same fabric on everything; you might use six or seven different fabrics. So it really is just like the inside but it's outside. We use chairs from Sutherlands, we also use a settee that is made using the new technology that lets rain go right through the upholstery. It's fabulous.

SUZANNE RHEINSTEIN Our porch, of course, has a blue ceiling. I've always thought it was for the sky, but my friend said it was to keep the flies out. I think that was a little bit of Southern lore she was telling me.

LIBBY CAMERON I worked on a plantation house in South Carolina. The original house was built in 1791 on the Sampit River. The records of the house were lost during the Civil War, so my client had a very difficult time getting a permit, but he prevailed and restored the house. He added electricity, plumbing, and bathrooms, and installed beautiful, very symmetrical formal gardens. When you drive up to the house today, there is a relatively modest portico on the front. The house faces rice fields and the river. There is a wonderful, deep, continuous porch, which begins at one corner on the front of the house and wraps around on three sides to the other corner on the front. It is filled with big deep Aiken sofas and has lots and lots of Charleston green-painted wicker. The floor slopes and after the plants have been watered, the water dribbles down to the edge and drips off onto the ground below. The floorboards are wide and run the full depth of the porch. The view is lovely; the rice fields are on the bank of the river so when the wind blows, you get clear views of it. It is one of the most wonderful and delightful places to sit. The proportions of the porch are perfect.

BRIAN McCARTHY Porches are absolutely essential to any good house. You need to have a space outdoors, whether it's a screened-in porch or just an open porch. I think that the width has to be a minimum of fifteen feet in order to accommodate enough furniture, to get a dining table, a sofa, and enough chairs to make it an outdoor living room.

It depends on where you are whether you are going to want screens or not. If you're going to live out there, ceiling fans are essential.

SUZANNE TUCKER I love the sound of wooden porches. There is a very specific kind of porch sound that you get with shingled or clapboard houses—that creak when you step on a loose board and that clear, hollow clack of your feet. It depends on where you are and the climate and how you are going to use them whether they need to be screened-in or not. In California we're lucky because we don't have that many bugs, so you don't have to have screens. I think they need to be furnished so that they are inviting. You really want to linger on a porch, to live on it.

MUD ROOMS AND CUTTING ROOMS OFTEN ACT AS MIDWAY STATIONS BETWEEN THE INSIDE AND OUTSIDE OF A HOUSE.

JEFFREY BILHUBER I dream of my porches. I am adding porches to this house I am renovating in the country. I have kind of flipped it around so what used to be the back garden is now the front of the house and I am realigning how you access the house, so I can get a garden back and get these two porches on.

Nancy Powers. I don't know if you have ever worked with Nancy Powers, who is a landscape designer. She is so great. She is out of Santa Barbara, and she did two of the greatest gardens I have ever known. She did David Easton's house upstate, which I loved. She did beautiful gardens in Santa Barbara. I was just fortunate enough to be able to ask her to help me. I am scared to death of siting a pool—I don't know how to do that. There is no second-guessing or moving it. I can drag the sofa in and out of the house all day long, but I am not digging a hole and putting a pool in without talking to someone who really understands the impact of that. I have dreams of vegetable gardens, and napping under trees, and sitting on porches, and scouring the East Coast for slightly dilapidated wicker furniture to jam onto both porches.

LIBBY CAMERON I have spent time with Albert on his porch in Southport. It was very simple, screened in with beige canvas and green and white leafy pillows, wooden furniture, and wicker. You looked out at his garden, which was very symmetrical; it had a round planting in the middle. There was a mercury glass sphere on a pedestal, which emphasized the balance of the garden. It was very pretty and filled with boxwood, hosta, and rhododendrons—there were very few flowers that I remember. The porch was very simple with Albert's wonderful objects on the tables; it felt very safe and calm. His porch felt more like a background or backdrop for the garden. It was the comma between the house and the garden.

EMMA BURNS My approach to gardens is similar to my approach to a house. I like to treat it as another room or as an extension of the house. I prefer a formal structure with soft planting within that. I like gardens to have different areas, different "rooms." I was hugely influenced by the garden at Sissinghurst.

BRIAN McCARTHY I love structures in the garden. I love pergolas; architectural elements in a garden are very important. Again, it goes back to your skyline: you also want to create skylines in the garden, in terms of what you are looking at from inside and to create a framework outside, so everything doesn't read at one level. Some people may want this wide, open expanse, but there is something so nice about creating intimacy in the garden.

EMMA BURNS It is such fun to peek around a corner to find another area. I like gardens to have different spaces that you can use at different times of the day. It's lovely to have a table where you can get the sun in the morning, where you can have breakfast or coffee. In my house in the country, I have a bench under a fig tree and that is the perfect place to have cocktails in the evening. At the very end of the garden there is a gazebo, which is just great at a certain time of the day. It's the way you use the house at different times and having a nice sort of balance between the bits of garden: more formal around the house and getting wilder farther away. I adore very natural planting, wildflowers and long grass. I find that very pretty. I like a limited palette of color in a garden; I love plants with a smell and I think that every garden, however small, should have water.

PORCH STYLE

There is no reason why people can't have comfortable porches.

BUNNY WILLIAMS

TODD ROMANO There is nothing I love more in the spring than a porch. Again that's the Texas boy in me. When I first moved here, I was taken to a house on Shelter Island that had such charm and taste, it left an indelible impression on me. My friend had a screened-in porch with wonderful wicker and rattan furniture, a big coffee table and a big drinks table, a screen in one corner, and floor lamps and table lamps. They used it literally as an outdoor living room. It was one of the most charming things I have ever seen. I love porches. I love furniture on porches. I love lighting outside.

Nowadays there are so many indoor-outdoor fabrics. There are almost too many. You can find something like a velvet that's an indoor-outdoor fabric—do you know that one, from Lee Jofa? You can really loft it up outside if you want to. I also love the idea of indoor-outdoor entertaining. I don't think there is anything nicer than sitting outside at the end of the day on a porch or a terrace in comfortable furniture, or having lunch on a big old porch. It really is wonderful, and it's a very important place. If you don't have an affinity for the garden or the outdoors, I think it gets overlooked. My friend has the most amazing terrace off of her pool room—in between her pool room and the rose garden. We have breakfast there, we have lunch there, and sometimes we'll have dinner there in the evening. It is so gorgeous to be outside and to eat a meal in the fresh air. I don't know. I love porches—love, love, love porches.

SUZANNE RHEINSTEIN Our porch is furnished: it has a table and chairs where you can eat; it has an Aiken sofa piled with pillows; it has two very old wicker chairs that I've had forever. It's all painted green, which brings it

LOVELY OLD GARDEN GATES AT THE END OF A STONE PATH.

together. One thing I usually do is a color scheme of anything that is outdoors. Our own color scheme, which has been the same for ten years, is green, which is what our shutters are, as well as all of the wood on the back. There are planter boxes that are French and they are stained this chartreuse color. Then there is the green, and the table that is striped chartreuse, and I have some old benches that are green and they are upholstered in chartreuse upholstery. It's a kind of nice way to bring a thread to the different things that you might see. I don't really like all those matching sets. My Aiken sofa is made with a twin mattress and it sits on our back porch, where we pretend to read the Sunday paper; those sofas were all throughout the South. I built one for the back of our house. I don't have lamps but I do have about thirty lanterns.

SUSAN BARTLETT CRATER You have to be careful not to ruin porches with that overly prissy Americana treatment, which always looks too feminine to me. *Fussy* is not a word you want to associate with outdoor decorating. The most stylish porch I have ever seen is at the house of a friend of ours in Maine. The house and adjoining porch, which overlooks the ocean, are painted a strong dark brown color and, beside the very simple black painted wicker, there are only masses of bright red geraniums. It is the contrast of the dark house, the red flowers, and the ocean that creates such an impact. Our friend likes to serve a very formal tea in the afternoon on the porch, which further compounds the striking simplicity of the setting.

One other important rule of thumb with porches was recently included in a *New York Times* article on exterior decorating by the architect and interior designer Benjamin Noriega-Ortiz. He aptly said that "the key to an interesting and fun outdoor space is never buy matching sets of anything." How many screened-in porches are dulled down by the matching set of catalog white wicker and nothing else? You don't want a fussy porch, but at the same time there are so many wonderful, unexpected old drink trolleys, day beds, antique lanterns, and eccentric planters, for example, that will make the porch more inviting and comfortable. We cherish our summer living, so why not make it a little more interesting?

LIBBY CAMERON Every piece of furniture in our house in Maine has at least six coats of paint on it. It's "cottage furniture," the name used for summer-house furniture. It isn't worth a great deal, and it usually consists of a myriad of shapes and textures—wood, wicker, iron, and more whimsical pieces. Hopefully all of the pieces are united by the color they have been painted. That coat of paint relinquishes the fussiness, but none of the charm.

It's extraordinary to think of what is now available for outdoor spaces, covered or not. Years ago I remember having fabric vinylized so it could be used outside. Most people wanted more than just the basic canvas stripes and colors that Sunbrella used to make. Now the choices are many, with patterns and the types of fabrics that you would use indoors—in fact, many people do use them inside if they have young children. But wicker was wicker when I was little, and it got painted every year. After the rain, it would have a springy feel to it. It's amazing to think that wicker, which is actually paper on a wood frame, can last as long as it does. Aside from the tiny nails that pop up and the scratchy edges it can get from too much sanding and paint, it is really very comfortable and so wonderful to look at.

I still love the unexpected on a porch and the odd pieces you can use as planters. In my grandparents' house in Maine, Mrs. Parish used old tires as planters for the front porch, which at first thought sounds ghastly, but somehow someone was able to turn the tires inside out and clip the edges in a zigzag pattern—as if cut by pinking shears, making the points stand out like a jester's cap. They were painted white and then filled with a variety of flowers—you really couldn't tell they were tires. They were very whimsical.

BUNNY WILLIAMS I just got rid of the last of the wicker by my pool because it was the real thing and it just collapsed. Nobody loves wicker more than I do, but it does not stand up if you have a porch that gets rained on. It stands up if you can keep it dry, but on an open porch that really gets a lot of rain, it falls apart. If you have a porch, there is so much great furniture that is plastic and looks fantastic. We have this new wicker at Treillage that looks like woven willow, and when you touch it, you think it is. We found it in Paris and

AN OLD BARREL IS A CHARMING CONTAINER FOR FLOWERS.

it's phenomenal. I just put it up in Connecticut and it looks fabulous, and it can get rained on.

A porch should be very serene and have a feel to it that is almost in between your house and the garden. The colors should be green and beige and found in the garden. I want to feel that I am in the garden already, and hate the use of pink and rose chintzes and American flags. It is a room, but it is still, to me, a garden. It should be simple. It should be appropriate—the bridge between the inside and the outside. I don't want anything there that keeps me from looking out at the garden or the lawn. I almost think of it as more of an extension of the garden than of the house. I think too many people try to make their porch look like another living room, and it's not.

PETER DUNHAM I entertain much more outside because I don't really have a very successful dining room situation inside. I can't stand the smell of cooked food inside. I guess everyone has their own thing. My friend had these really cool lampshades made for outside, a completely plastic lampshade that goes on a regular lamp. I love that because the lighting outside is always tricky—it's either too dark or too light. You can't read outside at night, and then the bugs come, of course. But there's always this lighting issue—there's either too much or too little.

Well, obviously, you have to use a lot of sconces on the walls. If I've got to have something hanging above, then I'll use hanging lanterns. But that always seems to me a big challenge—how to build up enough light, maybe trying to do a lot of lighting that's hidden within trees to give a certain amount of ambient light. Obviously, if I am entertaining, there are just a trillion candles and lanterns and hurricanes and torches hanging in the trees.

There are so many charming, whimsical things for outside that you can have fun with that you can't use inside. I'd rather it be like a garden, but there is also a level of practicality that you have to be aware of. If it rains once and the rug is out, what are you going to do—run out and get it?

DANIEL ROMUALDEZ If I am lucky enough to have a client with a great porch, I like to make it look like a second living room. I am doing a porch now and we are using not just wicker but also upholstered sofas. The space is glassed in but it really is a porch. My fantasy porch would have lamps. You would need to weight them somehow and make them out of something that wouldn't get destroyed. I just love the feeling of indoor living outdoors. We are doing a tea house, with curtains, and installing an outdoor TV. We are painting a rug on the floorboards.

THE COURAGE
to DECORATE

THE BRILLIANT COLOR SCHEME OF SISTER PARISH'S LIVING ROOM AT
960 FIFTH AVENUE WAS ENHANCED BY THE WHITE UPHOLSTERED FURNITURE
SET AGAINST THE GLOSSY AUBERGINE WALLS.

If you have what Sister often referred to as "courage," you can be the architect or engine of any number of great approaches to your first house or apartment with just a few cans of wonderful paint, a good imagination, and the willingness to mix it up with what you have been given to date. When my husband and I bought a house in the suburbs after we were first married, I couldn't wait to start painting and making it my own. My grandmother had recently died, but I felt her presence every step of the way. After my first of many visits to the local paint store, I studied all the paint chips I had chosen. In choosing the bold colors, I remembered her unstoppable style and confidence. "Never spend time looking for a place to park," she advised me. "Always drive directly to the front door and there will be room." Filled with energy from the purchase of a new house, it did not take me long to choose colors and start making the rooms my own.

Keeping in mind Sister's reliance on color to compensate for any number of weaknesses, I began with the library as I knew that is where Sister would say we would "live" because of its fantastic light. Building around two red and white upholstered chairs from Sister's last New York apartment, I painted the walls a brilliant blue. A little too brilliant, I thought, as I frantically called my mother. "I am in the library, Mom, and I feel like I'm calling from a lawn chair at the bottom of a David Hockney swimming pool." My mother, who is a beautiful artist herself, and knows her paint, recommended putting on a thin veneer of linen white to soften it or "muck it up" a bit. Working with a dry brush, I did just that and, after many hours of fooling with it, the color softened and looked like it had been there forever. As my mother had already predicted, sometimes the best results emerge from what at first appear to be unmitigated disasters.

I then hung red, blue, and green Moroccan valances, which Sister had picked up on her travels and given to me, over our library's arched doorways. They had a circuslike, almost gypsy look to them, which added the whimsical and unexpected element to the room. The valances, along with an old desk from Maine, and the masses of books my husband and I had accumulated over the years added memories of past rooms that I have loved. Finally, we hung our collection of animal paintings. These paintings are mostly dogs with a few odd sheep, cows, and pigs thrown in. I then placed a surly-looking red wooden parrot on a perch on the side of a window frame and we had our animal collection in place. With a faded English rug that has red roses in a grid pattern, a blue-and-white-checked sofa from Pottery Barn, brightly striped Alan Campbell pillows, and other odd bits of furniture, the room was done. Sitting back in the paint-spattered uniform I was to wear the first few months we lived in the house, I knew Sister had been with me and would have been very happy sitting in the sunlit room. The dominant force that energized me through the painting and decoration of this house was pleasure. The house had many deficiencies and we had no money for new projects or furniture, but it was so much fun to make it our own and look forward to the good times we would have in it.

A first house or apartment can be one of the most memorable places you will live as you have to rely on your imagination and creativity the most. Buying an old beat-up dining room table and covering it with an amazing vintage tapestry from a flea market can many times be more satisfying and more fun than the later purchase of a "serious" table. Not only is the challenge to make a great room with little money enticing, but the things you buy at that point in your life generally end up somehow having the most significance.

—SUSAN BARTLETT CRATER

DECORATING on a SHOESTRING

Have you ever considered how much pure stuff and nonsense surrounds this subject of interior decoration? Probably not. Almost everybody believes that there is something deep and mysterious about it or that you have to know all sorts of complicated details before you can lift a finger. Well, you don't.

DOROTHY DRAPER, *Decorating Is Fun*

MILES REDD The glorious thing about decoration is that you can do it cheaply. The apartment that I had in college was featured in *House Beautiful.* It was on 6th Street between Avenues B and C and shortly after I graduated I went to work for John Rosselli. I was twenty-one and I lived in that apartment for two years. Everything I had there was from a flea market or I had painted it or done it myself. I painted every surface, including the floor, which was green and vanilla white with a big-scale diamond design, very English conservatory. There was a little kitchen that was chocolate brown with red doors and white trim. The bedroom was striped and I painted the stripes myself. It was a taupey silvery beige and white. The living room was a celadon green with the green-and-white floor. I found two green velvet club chairs at a flea market, and they were there with a small red sofa and lots of artwork littering the walls. It had books and mirrors and trays with liquor bottles, which add warmth, and there was also something pretty and green, like a maidenhair fern. It was a great apartment and a wonderful design laboratory for me.

BUNNY WILLIAMS The very first apartment I lived in after I got married had a library. I went out and got a taxi-cab-yellow-and-brown print fabric that was like $20 a yard. Remember Far Eastern Fabrics? It was this wonderful hand-blocked Indian fabric and I upholstered the walls in the library with it. I did it myself, figured out how to do it! It had rattan bookcases from Pier One

and a convertible sofa bed because that had to be our extra guest bedroom. It was a chic room. It also had a straw carpet, but it was the bright-yellow-and-brown print walls that made it fun. I still love that room—I can still see it. The print compensated for the fact that I didn't have anything. I didn't really have any art. I didn't have any good furniture and I think the TV was in the bookcases. So color can make a statement. It makes you feel good.

MARIO BUATTA I lived in an apartment above Swifty's in 1962 and it was really the first place I lived in the city. It was an L-shaped walk-up on the top floor and there were three windows facing Lexington Avenue. The bathroom was decorated in that it had blue walls and an El Morocco fabric shower curtain and citron yellow towels. I still have all of it from 1962, do you believe that? The L-shaped room was a beautiful eggplant color and the chintz was a floral bouquet, which Sister copied from me.

MITCHELL OWENS My first true grown-up apartment—meaning one I didn't share with a roommate—was in Dallas, Texas, back in the mid-1980s. I was twenty-three then, and though I was working as the senior editor at a shelter magazine, I had very little money, as I recall. The building, however, was wonderful, a 1920s apartment block called The Argyle, and the rooms were relatively spacious and well laid out. It wasn't cookie cutter or cheap and the apartments had lovely parquet floors, nothing special mind you, but they were sensitively preserved.

I remember the sitting room was sparsely decorated since I didn't own much and couldn't really afford anything. At an antiques warehouse north of the city, I found a circa-1900 set of button-tufted furniture covered in its original dark green velvet and trimmed with bullion fringe the same color: a huge Chesterfield sofa with two hulking armchairs for a man and a woman, all of which cost $300, not including delivery. For $150, I snatched up two large

MILES REDD'S FIRST APARTMENT IN NEW YORK EXEMPLIFIES WONDERFUL AND IMAGINATIVE DESIGN POSSIBILITIES ON A LIMITED BUDGET.

vintage kilims from a showroom closeout sale, both rather large and colored madder red, chartreuse green, acid yellow, and dull white—those went on the sitting room's floor. The television and stereo went into an impressively tall stripped-pine armoire (I think that cost $200), and I made the room a bit more mysterious and cozy by partially enclosing the end closest to the front hall with a mediocre but substantially scaled Victorian folding screen made of fake Cordoba leather, edged with masses of nailheads. I painted the walls a very pale shade of adobe, sort of a warm sandy pink—it was Texas, after all, and it felt right with the furnishings I assembled.

LIBBY CAMERON I did an apartment for a young couple, just married in New York. He was very successful so the budget was not as restricted as those of most first apartments. Being a new bride, she was very careful not to be extravagant or cavalier in her choices of materials or fabrics. The apartment was full of color—a yellow living room, a pale blue bedroom, a toile guest room, and a soft green dining room. It's amazing how far you can get with color when other elements are missing. It was a happy apartment and perfect for just the two of them. It was great fun working with her as she was new to the process, very curious, and asked good questions. She didn't have any collections or preconceived ideas of what the apartment should be. We went to Sotheby's and Christie's to find furniture, and downtown where the antiques district used to be based. She learned a lot and really wanted to understand the process.

SUSAN BARTLETT CRATER Albert Hadley's first apartment is the one I have heard the most about, which is no surprise. Bill Hodgins gave me the best description of it.

WILLIAM HODGINS Remember that beautiful silver room he had? It was one of the most beautiful, quietly dazzling rooms ever. It was square with high ceilings and the walls had silver foil paper on them, so it just glittered. I remember he had all linen-covered furniture, four very beautiful big chairs. You know he was always into that plaster furniture. And then there were some emerald green glasses and other objects in this room. And on the floor was wall-to-wall thick woven raffia. Remember that? God, it was beautiful. The next time I met Mrs. Parish, she was sitting there with her Jack Daniel's.

LIBBY CAMERON We lived in a loft in New York. It was a huge space with twelve-foot-high ceilings and had rooms at either end. There were windows on all sides so it was always bright and light. I was at Parish-Hadley at that point, creating rooms with intimacy and coziness—

the antithesis of what our loft was about, but I solved that issue. I arranged the space in such a way that there were four seating areas, and a big tall mirrored screen that reflected the living area back onto itself, making it feel warmer and not quite so big. It was all really quite neutral—with creamy white sofas, spotted leopard chintz on the chairs, a dusty blue and beige screen behind the biggest sofa, a blue-and-cream-striped Dhurrie rug, cream-colored lamps and walls, and very, very dark floors. There was a round table with a chocolate brown-and-white tablecloth, a baby grand piano, and a blue-and-cream-colored wallpaper border around the ceiling line. The furniture shapes were relatively traditional and it didn't feel at all like what one imagines when you think of a loft. It was very serene and had big baskets for dress-up costumes and toys for the children.

LIBBY CAMERON UTILIZED COLOR AND AN ECLECTIC MIX OF FURNITURE TO CREATE A WARM AND INVITING SPACE IN HER LARGE LOFT IN NEW YORK.

SUSAN CRATER'S LIBRARY EMPHASIZES A MISHMASH OF FAMILY CASTOFFS
AND A COLLECTION OF FOLK ART PAINTINGS.

FIRST PURCHASES

Everybody thinks, "Oh, the Bride," and they go out and buy gold rim china and cut crystal and no one uses it, because we don't live that way anymore. We have to match what we buy with our lifestyle. BUNNY WILLIAMS

SUZANNE RHEINSTEIN You've just moved into this space and first you have to decide if you are going to be a color person or a neutral person in this instance. If you're a neutral person, that's pretty simple as you can have it done with a beige or white slipcover and a sisal rug. After that you can get two lamps and concentrate on what kind of art you like, and maybe splurge on one thing. Put up bamboo shades to start and then later you can put up white linen or beige curtains. This gives you a very neutral palette, then you can figure it out from there. For example, you can have all your books in the living room: what could be better than tons of books and everything else is white. You'll start collecting things.

Also, you can add big dramatic plants with green leaves and, of course, there is a lot of great wicker out there. If you take the simple kind of wicker and mix it up—put it around your dining room table and then have a table that looks scrubbed. I would love a beach house like that. That's one way you can go.

Let's continue with a person who wants more color in a first apartment. You have begged, borrowed, or stolen a sofa and you're going to upholster it—not in a print, but in a great color you love and you're going to have it piped in another color. Then you're going to find some chairs and put something on those and then you're going to find an étagère and you're going to have it spray-painted a great color and that will give you some height. Then you can get some posters or maybe frame wallpaper, which I think is interesting. Also, of course, mirrors. Then get a sisal rug. You know you can get those for not much money in all the catalogues, and then there are all kinds of crafty things you can do to a sisal rug. You can paint a border on it, but don't get too crafty. I think you should concentrate on bigger things. Start with the color of the room, a sofa, and two chairs, then you need something to organize things. Most people have all that little stuff everyplace. You can take all that stuff and put it in the étagère.

ALBERT HADLEY Well, you can buy from the catalogues—if it's appropriate, it's okay. They have some very good designs, though it's not what you'd call the best quality. It's not going to last forever, but in a linear sense and in a design sense, there are some pieces that work.

TODD ROMANO If your clients have been fortunate enough to buy a space large enough—be it a house or an apartment, which they know they are going to be in for a very long time—then I encourage them to address all the structural, architectural, and construction issues first. Take care of the backdrop. If it's an older house or an older apartment, go ahead and spend the money to renovate it properly. If that means some rooms are left empty and you do it over a period of time, that's fine. I would rather see them do that so we never have to go back and address plumbing, bathroom, kitchen, or electrical issues. If they truly are starting out and it's a smaller apartment and I get the sense they are not going to stay there very long, we basically concentrate on buying and doing things that they can take with them to the next place. I had clients with this exact situation recently. Even though by New York standards they had a pretty nice apartment, I knew they wouldn't be there forever. So we concentrated on making wonderful upholstered furniture for them, buying great artwork, buying some very pretty antiques, and some great dining chairs. Things that I knew we would then be able to move to their next place. Sometimes we will even avoid major paint jobs because that might be a waste of money if they are going to move in two years. We will put the emphasis on "the Beverly Hillbillies" things they can load up on the back of their truck and take with them to the next place.

BUNNY WILLIAMS If you are going to do an all-white room, you better have some good things to put in it, because they are going to be very noticeable. I think people should try to buy the best they can. I still have the sofa that I had from my first apartment. It has been recovered a couple of times, but I still have it because it was a very good sofa. Sometimes we spend a lot of money on things that are cheap because that's all we can afford. Ultimately, because they are really cheap, they fall apart.

Instead I think people should try the second-hand shops and flea markets and hunt for things that have some age. Find things that were made at a time when things were made better—they will stand up. Also, and this is an old Sister Parish trick, there is a lot of furniture that has a great line to it and it is interesting, but it is ugly wood and so you paint it white. When you see really beautiful wood—you know, eighteenth-century faded mahogany—that's worth preserving, but 1950s sprayed lacquer red mahogany is not worth saving. You can get 1950s Ethan Allen furniture in a thrift shop or at a tag sale for nothing and paint it. You go to "Jones," which has what I call secondhand furniture, but all of a sudden you say that's a nice Queen Anne leg or that has a great look to it and paint it white. Suddenly, it looks fresh.

A RED RICKRACK TRIM ON A SIMPLE WHITE COTTON SLIPCOVER ADDS DETAIL TO AN OTHERWISE PLAIN AND SIMPLE CHAIR.

CATHY KINCAID Well, first of all, nothing is worth a divorce with a first apartment or house. If you just got married, there is a lot going on. Stay within your budget first thing. We do a budget estimate so it's all on paper. We don't order anything until someone sees exactly how much it is going to cost, and then they go through and pick and choose. The wife starts looking at everything on the budget and the husband goes to the last page and looks at the bottom line. Never, ever does he look at what it is—he looks at the bottom line and takes a deep breath and rolls his eyes. So the first thing you do is give them a budget of estimates and let them go through it and choose their priorities and plan to do it in phase 1, phase 2, and phase 3. However many phases it takes. Everyone has a budget, even if they are very wealthy.

You start with a good sofa, a good club chair. Buy one piece of furniture or a piece of art that you absolutely love, that just makes you happy and that you want to look at forever and ever. When I was first married, I bought a nine-foot pine table from an English antiques dealer in Dallas. I put it on layaway—it took me four months to pay for it and I still have it. I saw the dealer at a garden club talk that I did recently and she came up and asked me if I still had it. I used it in my office for a long time. It's just a great worktable, and then I bought a piece of art I absolutely love that I also still have. It's a Julio Larraz. He is a Cuban artist. It has a sunny yellow background with this big slice of a watermelon on a butcher-block table. My advice is to buy one thing that is a passion and for the rest just make things do.

SUZANNE TUCKER I would go antiquing with my mother when I got my first apartment after college, and other than hand-me-downs from my mother, that is what I used. This was the seventies, the era of great estate sales, and my mother would pick up things for me—flatware, a beautiful sideboard—and send them to me in LA. So I would have these great pieces. My father definitely had an influence on me as well. He was fifty-eight when I was born and he died at one hundred and two. So I had a much older male figure in my life, which was a great gift and a terrific luxury. I overheard him say to somebody in his later years, in his nineties, that I got all my taste from him. It was pretty funny that he was taking full credit. One of the things I remember distinctly about my father was that he loved good furniture and had a very good eye. When my parents sold their big house and got a smaller one, they wanted to get a beautiful crystal chandelier. There was a store in Pasadena that I knew had chandeliers and I wanted to see, so my father took me. We walked in and looked around until he said, "Which one do you like?" I told him which one and he bought it. I think I was eleven or twelve. Now granted, the chandelier was okay, but I realized later on what that did for me in terms of confidence. The fact that my father trusted my opinion enough to even ask me was powerful. I didn't know it at the time. I look back on that now and realize that was pretty amazing. My father had a lot of influence in that way. He really appreciated architecture and good homes.

If it's a first apartment I would say paint it a color that brings something to the space that has some punch and some fun to it. In terms of furniture, the first piece to buy would be the sofa. Invest in a sofa. It's pretty universal that it tends to be the biggest piece in the room and then you can add small pieces to it. Go to the flea market—we all lived with orange crate boxes as side tables. There is nothing wrong with that and it doesn't have to be perfect.

My advice to young people is go to the antiques shops and ask questions. Dealers love to talk about their pieces. Ask why something is this price, what makes it this price, what makes it special—and educate yourself so that you can start to understand. Don't ever be afraid you'll ask a stupid question.

INSPIRATION and EDUCATION

The more knowledge you have, the more successful the outcome.

JEFFREY BILHUBER

SUSAN BARTLETT CRATER Libby's house is one of the purest reflections of a personality that I know. It reflects her love of her children and family most of all, but also the importance of her animals, who are considered members of the family—at a minimum, four dogs (Tussah, Logan, George, and Maisie), two cats, rotating rabbits, guinea pigs, birds, and so on—and her gardens. It is the most wonderful, warm, eclectic mix of color, furniture, paintings, and objects you can imagine. Her living room is all yellows, her dining room a wonderful pink, and the library a bright blue. All are put together with a great flair, a sophisticated sense of comfort, and a dazzling approach to color. Not only are the rooms beautiful to look at, but they just work. She can entertain twenty or two at a moment's notice and, like Sister, somehow amazingly never seems rushed.

Her house is an example of that wonderful moment that occurs when someone has knowledge derived from experience, exposure, and education and can apply it to a project that has great significance for them—in this case, her own house. Libby has traveled all over the world. From grand horse-racing plantations in South Africa to stately London town houses, she clearly draws on a large background of knowledge, which has helped form her eclectic approach. Confidence and the capitalization of trusting one's instinct naturally emerge from exposure and curiosity, two trademarks of the great decorator, professional or amateur.

THE LIVING ROOM IN EVANGELINE BRUCE'S TOWN HOUSE IN LONDON WAS DECORATED BY JOHN FOWLER, WHO IS CONSIDERED ONE OF THE GREATEST INFLUENCES IN DESIGN TODAY.

LIBBY CAMERON When we decided to leave New York City, Cully and I decided on a fan-shaped search, from the Hudson River to the Long Island Sound, to find a location no farther than forty-five minutes by train to his office on Wall Street. We ended up in Larchmont, looked at six houses, and I fell for one of them. I don't think that I could begin to tell you what it was that struck me—it just felt right, though I do remember liking the flowers that the neighbor had planted along a path. Later that week, when our bid had been accepted, I was downtown shopping at Far Eastern Fabrics, which no longer exists. I can't remember what my mission was, but a piece of madras with colors I loved caught my eye, and by the time I got back to the office, I had figured out what our house would look like. One of the colors was a pinkish orange—almost the color of the drinks we got from Howard Johnson's when I was little. From that one snippet of fabric, I was inspired and had absolutely no qualms about anything that I was thinking of doing.

The house is quite boring and ordinary to look at from the front. Inside the front door is a small entry hall, with a living room to the right, the stairs directly in front of you, the dining room a smidge to the left and straight ahead. There was a dull brown pine-paneled library, which had no life, or energy, and brown wall-to-wall carpeting.

Brunschwig and Fils had a bold wallpaper border, which I loved, that had corals, blues, creams, and yellows in it—I wanted to use it in the little entry. I had done a guest room at the Kips Bay Show House the previous spring, and knew that I wanted to use that same "Serendipity" wallpaper with the blue stars. So I went to work, ripped out every shred of carpeting, painted the living room a butter yellow, and used the valances I had had made for the Kips Bay Show House on the windows that faced the road. I painted the library Bachelor's Button blue in a shiny finish, the dining room was the color of the drink from Howard Johnson's, and the kitchen was yellow, because I had leftover paint from the living room. I just did it—I did not blink an eye. There are strong bright colors in each room and without realizing it, the wallpaper border tied the entire first floor together—every room was a color from that border.

After the house was more or less put together, I invited Mrs. Parish, Albert

Hadley, and Alan Campbell for a Sunday lunch. Moments before they were due to arrive, the kids were still running around without any clothes on, the dogs had just eaten all of the French bread off the counter, and Cully hadn't come back yet from picking up more berries for dessert. The doorbell rang—it was Mrs. Parish and Alan—she was always very prompt. Mrs. Parish walked in and immediately said that she and Alan had to look around. I took the kids upstairs to get dressed and heard Cully come in, say hello, and offer them a drink—thank god. Flora and Charlotte came down, dressed, and said hello. Charlotte was showing Mrs. Parish and Alan her curtsy; she must have curtsied thirty times before I could persuade her to stop, but her audience loved it.

Albert had arrived from his country house and asked if he could peek around. I was feeling quite nervous at this point, but luckily lunch was ready, so we sat down. Mrs. Parish turned to Cully and said, "Your house is perfection. It feels just like Libby. It has a fey quality to it, and is just full of charm."

That was a really wonderful, funny lunch. Mrs. Parish and Albert regaled us with stories about working on a project on the West Coast. It was just one of those great times when everyone laughs and has fun. After lunch, they all headed back into the city. I went upstairs to see the girls, who had been very quiet. It turns out that they had been working very hard connecting the gold dots between the stars on the wallpaper while we were eating lunch.

TODD ROMANO They were asking Mrs. Paley why she was always so chic and so beautifully turned out, and she said, "Because I can afford to make mistakes." This I think goes hand in hand with the strength and the courage of people like Sister Parish or Dorothy Draper. Because not only did they have strength and conviction of their opinions, but they also did make mistakes, and through those mistakes they would learn. A lot of these people in the beginning were self-taught.

CARLETON VARNEY I will tell you a thing about Dorothy as a person. Cleveland Amory wrote a book about her, and in the interviews for the book she said she married George Draper to break out of the walls of Tuxedo Park.

Growing up as Paul Tuckerman's daughter, she was called Star and was educated only with private tutoring, as that's the way they did it. She traveled and lived within the confines of a prison, which is what she thought of Tuxedo Park. So in order to break out in those years—remember this was the twenties and there were no schools in interior design—she went to work. She was entirely self-taught. Dorothy Draper was a person who dwelled within her own mind.

SUSAN BARTLETT CRATER One of Sister's favorite lines was, "It is only my eye that has helped me" and, in many ways, that was true. She could barely draw and was hopeless with a scale ruler, but she had been exposed to some incredible houses in her youth and she continued to travel frequently as an adult. She was self-taught, but her eye had been influenced by the houses she had seen and lived in. She said she spent her first tour of Europe as a child "with her eyes squeezed shut," and that was probably true. I had a similar experience with her when I was twelve. She took me to England with Albert and Alan Campbell, and we toured Blenheim Palace and other great houses, but I took in little while they tried in vain to point things out to me. Luckily, by the time Sister's parents bought an apartment in Paris, she was ready to absorb the beauty around her.

She was a quick study and Mark Hampton told me her memory of the great houses she had seen was well known. She loved England and was a frequent visitor to London and the countryside. She was inspired by her friends' houses and the work of the firm Colefax and Fowler, with which she was briefly associated. Later she put her own imprint on the English look—mixing traditional English chintzes with American quilts and rag rugs. She frequently visited her old friend Nancy Lancaster, and her letters home were filled not only with details of Nancy's incredible taste, but also with tales of laughter and good friends—the mark of a wonderful house in her eyes. The letter she wrote to my grandfather from Ditchley, not long after the war, is indicative of what she drew from her frequent trips abroad. At that point Ronald Tree was living there with his new wife, Marietta, but the house had been worked on extensively by Nancy Lancaster when she had been married to Tree.

Darling Harry,

In your most fantastic dreams you could not imagine such beauty. Michael brought me down. We were met at Oxford in a beautiful dark blue car. The countryside is a mass of jonquils, bluebell blossoms, lush green fields, walled gardens with fruit trees climbing up the walls, rosy-cheeked children, thousands of bicycles (no cars), horses, and carts.

Ronnie and Marietta opened the door and I walked into the most fantastically beautiful house that I had ever hoped to see. You feel Nancy Lancaster in every corner. Room after room of such pieces, the way they are placed, the needlework carpets, crystal chandeliers—all candles, china—oh lord, it's terrific. First is the great hall (where we had high tea), the china room (silk walls), the velvet room (velvet red wall), then the green and white writing room, then stucco room, then library (50 feet long), then Ronnie's desk room, then large dining room, then breakfast room. Each is more perfect than the last. A good deal of the furniture was here from when it was built in 1700. The bedrooms are even better, if possible. All four-poster beds with crowned tops. In my room now I had a little stepladder (covered in white damask) to get up. The furniture is white lacquer with green jade! Each bath has a fireplace and such gems as needlework bath mats, beautiful consoles (as sinks), baskets of toilet paper with lavender bags—I could go on forever but I have no power of description.

Dinner something—fresh asparagus, four glasses of one thing or another, just the boys and the D'Elangers—great fun and laughter.

—SISTER PARISH FROM DITCHLEY

TODD ROMANO There are things you pick up through your experiences working with good people and there are things you pick up from your travels. I have always said I am only as good as the last piece of great furniture I have seen or the last great house I have been in.

PETER DUNHAM I see a lot of people in the States, who basically want to live in a hotel or have the look of a hotel. I think this comes because, and this is a really snobbish thing to say, the American experience is much more limited. I mean compared to England, where there is always kind of a fancy house in the country near where you grew up, even if you grew up in a little village. In Europe, at one point or another, you are exposed to these palettes and you see the pinnacle of the amazing beautiful chateaus in France or the great country houses in England. Whereas I grew up thinking my inspiration is Lord and Lady something or other, who had an incredible house with incredible colors and beautiful paintings and furniture and it was all mixed together, and it was kind of roses and seventeenth-century Chinese porcelain. A lot of people here want what they last saw at the Four Seasons Hotel.

EMMA BURNS Decorators in England have a great awareness and interest in the past and often reinvent and reinterpret it. If you think about how we at Colefax have worked with some of the same fabrics for years, yet in every single room where they are used the look is completely different. We have huge archives and libraries of books of fabrics and wallpapers and the joy of fumbling through those is amazing. We are also lucky enough to be working in such a great building that is full of reference points.

DAVID WEBSTER There are certain decorators (more seasoned decorators specifically) who come in and know the different periods of furniture. They know that that table is going to be perfect as a center table somewhere, or as a cocktail table, and they do not waffle in front of their clients. They come in and they point and they say this is it, this is what you need. Again, it's the whole confidence thing and salesmanship. I think that if you are confident and show

THE PRESIDENTIAL SUITE, A SEPARATE FREE-STANDING BUILDING AT THE GREENBRIER HOTEL, WAS CREATED BY THE ALLEGHANY CORPORATION ESPECIALLY FOR THE DUKE AND DUCHESS OF WINDSOR'S VISIT. DOROTHY DRAPER'S TREATMENT OF THE SUITE EMPHASIZED COLOR, DRAMATIC FLOURISHES, AND GLAMOUR. THE GREENBRIER HAS INSPIRED GENERATIONS OF DECORATORS.

your client you have the knowledge, they will be confident and you are going to do a great job in giving them the best of what they should have.

JEFFREY BILHUBER As a decorator I am just hitting my stride. I have been practicing my trade for twenty-plus years. It's just now that I really understand why all of these forms have existed over time and how some materials can do what you want them to do and how others might resist your temptation to try to make them into something else.

Understanding your craft and defining and implementing luxury—here we have a certain degree of working knowledge as to why things work and how they can work better that the consumer would not have. Why would they? We have hands-on daily engagement with all the materials, which gives us a leg up in the decision-making process.

PETER DUNHAM Books are really important and travel is very important. I need to be looking at books about Japanese temple architecture. I have thousands of books because that's one way to replenish yourself. You can find inspiration from multiple things: travel, of course; old films can really inspire you; and going to museums and seeing colors in artwork. Artists have so much more imagination and are way ahead of anyone else.

DANIEL ROMUALDEZ I worked at Bob Stern's office for five years and he had a great library. Whenever we would be working on a project we would have references and look at books. Because of that training, that's how we work here. What I end up doing when people have a question, even though I give them the answer, I say look at this and this, and you will see where my answer came from and that it's not just some arbitrary thing. It's like law; there are precedents for everything. You look things up and make sure you are on the right track. Obviously, you can do variations on all this and make it more original, but it has to be based on some rules.

ALBERT HADLEY Obviously, you can't have much of an opinion if you don't know anything about what you are talking about. You have to have some education or some exposure. I am always interested in young people who have some kind of knowledgeable background about the business and about the people who have been involved in it over the years. For instance, last week—it had nothing to do with a job—but Edward Cave had sent me a message saying that this young person was doing a book about Van Day Truex and would I talk to him, and I said of course. I had him come to my apartment because of the Truex drawings and the lamp and all that. Well he came and he was absolutely so far beyond that. He had obviously read Adam Lewis's book. He knows the name of everybody who has ever been involved in design. All of that helps. I find today that there are fewer and fewer young people who are aware of the people that have come before them and what's gone on in the world before them.

At our office I look for individuals who have some knowledge of the history and the background of our business. Architecture is part of it, but not all of it. At the least they should know who the people were who were doing the important work early in the twentieth century, starting back with Edith Wharton and Elsie de Wolfe and all the lady decorators. When I was growing up, I was educated mainly from magazines because in those days that's where you could get at it. All of the magazines were so fabulous because they showed how the best of the best people lived—the ladies and gentlemen of style and taste, and what their houses looked like. The articles were wonderful and many of the magazines in the thirties had marvelous illustrations by the artist of the day. They showed Billy Baldwin's work in full color in sketch form—I was looking at them in Nashville just a couple of weeks ago.

JOHN ROSSELLI To become educated, the best thing is to go back and read; there are so many books. There are so many early- or mid-century *House & Garden* or *House Beautiful* publications, for example. First off, you have to have a desire to learn. You have to be interested in going and viewing the auctions and studying the auction catalogs. Going to the bookstore, going to flea markets in New York. Doing the shops uptown and downtown. Don't be afraid of going into the shops and saying, "Hello, I am studying to be an interior decorator or I am going to school, do you mind if I look around?" Most shopkeepers will say fine and be happy to answer questions.

BUNNY WILLIAMS My first inspiration to become a designer came when I was thirteen and my parents took me to the Greenbrier Hotel, which Dorothy Draper had just finished decorating. Friends of theirs were investors so we went there for lunch. I just couldn't believe it. I had never seen cabbage roses that big on the floor and it was just fabulous—absolutely fabulous. We had lunch there and a tour of the Presidential Suite, and I kept thinking, what fun it would be to put all of this together.

You know what was great about it—coming from a fairly conservative life—you know everybody in Charlottesville had oriental rugs and English furniture and horse pictures. The Dorothy Draper style was—well, the lobby had cabbage rose carpet and emerald green—it was very decorated and for me it was like—you just couldn't believe it. It was overblown, exciting, dramatic, and theatrical. I think that was pretty avant garde for the Waspy set, who were running the decorating world at that time. You might have chintz and an oriental rug and a blue wall and English furniture. So this was pretty over the top, but magical in the best possible way. I could hear my mother going, boy, this is a bit . . . I could hear my parents thinking it was a bit much and me thinking, boy, this is it! She was better at doing public spaces than private spaces. Her style was best in her amazing public places.

I was very lucky to grow up in a family with members that lived not too far from one another. Everybody also loved their houses. There were no restaurants so everybody was at home. I had a cousin Josephine who had a house with wonderful painted Italian furniture and it looked so different. I had the luck of seeing people who lived well, and it was not that their houses were the grandest, but they really knew how to live in them. They had parties all the time; they cared about them. My godmother's living room had a beautiful Aubusson carpet. It was the idea that decorating—because I think for me and I think for you—is about creating a home. I am not trying to create a stage-set. I am not trying to create something just to make a pretty picture. I am really trying to create a place that people are going to do something in.

MILES REDD I always tell people to read all the books and all the magazines—get a subscription to *The World of Interiors*. There may be an article on the Duchess of Devonshire and then an article on some modernist. There is a real perspective of a wide range of design, and it's intelligently written about. As far as my inspiration, there are so many. But as a very little boy I admired the houses the architect Philip Trammell Shutze designed in Atlanta. He was a great kind of David Adler of Atlanta and built this Italian house. It was a huge inspiration to me as a child, but then as I came along and started reading and figuring things out, I would say David Adler, Albert Hadley, Bunny Williams, Billy Baldwin, Bill Blass, Oscar de la Renta, Dorothy Draper, and William Haines. Also, Cedric Gibbons, who did all the sets in Hollywood. My inspiration was largely a lot of movies—*The Fountainhead, Inside Daisy Clover*. I don't know if you ever saw that film with Natalie Wood, where she sings in the movie, which is a little like—turn it down—but the sets are Hollywood Regency. Have you ever seen *How to Murder Your Wife*? That house is just madly chic. I love Colefax and Fowler and Nancy Lancaster and Cecil B. It's endless. I feel like I have taken something from everyone and we haven't even talked about fashion editors and fashion photographers. Richard Avedon—I love his photographs from 1947 to 1977, even though there is not one interior. They evoke a mood that I love to capture. Walter Day, Picasso, always Sargent. Everything is inspiration to me.

FOLLOWING YOUR INSTINCTS

You do have to trust your instinct and your first instinct is usually the right instinct.   BRIAN McCARTHY

SUSAN BARTLETT CRATER Working in different venues, Dorothy Draper and Sister both capitalized on the confidence they drew from their backgrounds and, in many ways, worked on pure instinct, creating bold and innovative design. One of Dorothy Draper's most successful projects was the Arrowhead Springs Hotel, one of the most popular hot spots for movie stars in the 1940s. The hotel was a huge commercial success, in large part because of Draper's bold use of color, attention to detail, and glamorous design schemes.

In the November 2008 issue of *Architectural Digest* writer Gerald Clarke recently paid tribute to the incredible legacy of Draper as embodied in this fantastically successful hotel.

> *Bold, bolder, boldest was her operating philosophy. As far as she was concerned, the ebony columns in the lobby were not just there to hold up the ceiling. Almost as impressive as those in the Temple of Karnak, they informed guests they had arrived at a very special place. . . . In the world Draper created, a door was not merely a door. It was a portal to adventure.*

Ultimately, Sister felt that really good decorators were either born with it or they weren't. She did not feel you could go to school for decorating. Certainly, you could see a lot of great houses and apprentice and be trained, but, in her

A BEDROOM IN THE PALAZZO CORSINI IN ROME. THE SCALE OF THE BED IS APPROPRIATE TO THE PALAZZO'S GRAND ARCHITECTURE AND CEILING HEIGHTS.

mind, it was imagination that separated the good from the great. Like with any art medium, copying is, of course, never as good as the original. Although she certainly drew from her past and was inspired by others, she also reinterpreted and did not copy like so many decorators do. Her work was original and her imagination and instincts made it so.

BRIAN McCARTHY You need to go with your gut, and if something just reaches out to you, just step up to the plate and trust that that's the right thing to do. I find very often when clients backpedal it waters down the whole final effect. It then becomes confusing for them and they start to second guess and lose the clarity.

TODD ROMANO You can learn who the good upholsterers are and why they are good, and you can learn what height a club chair needs to be and how high the arms should be and what pitch the back should be, but it all goes back to the eye. I had probably the greatest compliment of my life from Albert. We were talking about this one day, and we were talking about the differences between what you can learn in school and what you can learn in training and what you have in you. Albert said to me, and I'm bragging now—I am just going to brag because I will never forget it, especially because he said, "Baby," and you know how he says "baby"—he goes, "But baby, you've the eye and you have to have that to be really good."

MILES REDD I think that decorating takes a certain visual confidence. You can teach and teach it, but not necessarily learn it. Someone can teach me algebra until I am blue in the face and I can say it back and regurgitate it, but does it ever sink in? I try not to make too many rules because then I think you get boxed in. There is perfection in imperfection, that's what I always say. You want some things to be a little off.

CAROLYN ENGLEFIELD Real personal style is knowing who you are and how you want to live. Someone who is not afraid, but confident in their own taste—comfortable creating it and living with it, as well as enjoying it and sharing the experience with others.

WILLIAM HODGINS Besides the sort of technical things of decorating and learning what to do and what things not to do and ways of looking at rooms, Mrs. Parish gave to me quite a bit of confidence. I think that made a big difference to me because I really was very shy. I was like a fifteen-year-old instead of a twenty-five-year-old. It is so important to feel a certain amount of strength and confidence. Certainly Madam gave that to me and I didn't have it before.

LIBBY CAMERON Mrs. Parish was really the person who gave me confidence. She believed in me. We were close friends and she taught me a lot, not only about decorating but about the value of close friendships and family and traditions. She was funny and she was real and, for whatever reason, she made me feel like I was doing the right thing. She was amazing in that way. She didn't take that many people under her wing, but when she liked you, she liked you and that was that.

SUSAN BARTLETT CRATER The other type of confidence that can make a great house is the courage to trust a great decorator. The really good ones will only appreciate the job all the more if their client has knowledge, curiosity, and the desire to learn. Most important, however, is trust. A truly inspired house, where a great decorator's seen or unseen hand is the most unforgettable, is one where the client has given the decorator full rein.

ALBERT HADLEY This business requires total involvement. It has to do with giving them what they never knew they wanted. That's our job, but you have to know what your clients are about. The more sophisticated and the more knowledgeable they are, the more satisfying it is to us as professionals. That doesn't mean they have to know where the fabrics come from or how much they cost. Forget that; cost should be out of the picture as a learning process.

You don't consider money at all. If you're focusing on how much money you are going to make, then you're not designing properly.

JEFFREY BILHUBER Anna Wintour wrote the forward of my first book, and she said something, which is very true, not only about me, but about any great decorator. She said, "Jeffrey is the sort of decorator who takes your own taste and makes it better. That's what really good decorating is going to do." Great decorating is nothing more than great communicating.

PETER DUNHAM I think the layperson is going to do what comes naturally to them, which is probably similar to their parents. When you hire a designer, that designer should be pushing your envelope. They should be saying okay, I know you love pink, but I think black would look really good on you. You would think, oh no, I never wear black. You start hammering at them to just try it. I think that that is the role of the decorator—you have to push people. Basically you are bringing together the husband and the wife—so already you have to be a diplomat—and then you have to realize that they likely bought a house that isn't actually what they wanted, but it happened to be in the right location and it was the right price. And they didn't really realize they didn't like it quite as much as they thought. You have to make the house work and the two of them work. Then you have to try to have fun and make it interesting. Take some risks and make it happen. I find if I'm sort of churning out the same thing that I did for somebody else just because it's easy and I want to get out the door—I'm really kind of depressed and bored—I'm like, whatever. But I'm much more excited if my juices are going and I know we can do that thing that I have always wanted to do. This is the project that I can do it on. I try to get them to go either to buy or to educate their eye. It's tough. People don't necessarily want to go to college with you. They want you to do it.

I think you have to try to take as much as you can of their magic. Like my clients from Woodside, this amazingly intelligent couple who are completely different from anything else I have experienced. They made a lot of money on video games and they are just intelligent. So I started talking to them and

I discovered that after they had left the University of Virginia, where they met and got married, they sold everything and went to India for a year. I was like, wow, that's amazing. That gives me a lead into the decorating. I say, "Okay, let's make that room your Indian hippie and make that part of your experience." You have to pull these things out of people. You try to find something that will make the house a reflection of them.

EMMA BURNS Sometimes you have people who specifically say I want you to push me, push me, which is huge fun. I enjoy offering radical solutions. I love to block up windows if they are in the wrong place and it means we would create a proper wall for the room. We don't have any light, anyway. I really enjoy kind of suggesting things. I mean the decorator is not there to be a yes person. You help by editing people's taste. Some of the clients I have worked with a lot say they see me as an editor of their taste, that they enjoy working with me because they feel that, with my help, they will achieve a much better house.

AN ENGLISH STANDING LAMP WITH A SILK BOX-PLEATED SHADE LIGHTS A SIMPLE SLIPPER CHAIR WITH A CHARTREUSE GREEN SLIPCOVER.

PAUL VINCENT WISEMAN I have pep talks at my firm. I get everybody together and ask: "How many hats can you wear?" These kids come out of school or wealthy families that don't teach them anything about working. I tell them "Paul Vincent Wiseman does windows." They watch me on an installation. I'm under the table wiping things down—doing whatever it takes. How many hats can you wear and not have any attitude about it. We're in a business where you come in the front door sometimes, but the back door most of the time. No attitude and don't get upset if you didn't get invited to the big party. Usually you're going out the door just before the party comes. In Sister's generation, they were in trade and we are in trade. Don't fool yourself. Most of the people with the money don't have much sophistication themselves, anyway. That's part of our job. There is poverty at that level now because wealth comes so quickly, there is no culture that comes with it. Do you have that book *Dictators' Homes*? I gave it to a bunch of my clients for Christmas last year. It has a leopard cover and shows homes of real dictators. I gave it to select clients and they got the joke. I say to my clients, "We will get along really fine if you memorize these three things: (1) We're not saving lives—it's only decorating. (2) It's not a product; it's a process. And (3) In very fine print on the back of my card it says, it gets here when it gets here." I try to make them laugh and to see the humor in it. We are creating something for them; it's about them, not about me.

JEFFREY BILHUBER The creative process is a fleeting flash. In great decorating, it's really 85 percent follow-up. The creativity comes in a moment of great communication and great inspiration and then you come up with these great pictures and great ideas. The rest of it is just follow-up. It's being able to deliver on the dream. Being able to actually transfer what only I can see into three-dimensional realities. That takes work.

PETER DUNHAM You have to deal with people's mood. I know it took me a long time to learn this and I hope I pass this wisdom along to younger designers. The worst times for me were the times when I was impatient, when the client decided they didn't want to do something that I wanted really badly and I couldn't let go of it. It was very painful. It's much better to concede something and let go, and if they don't get it right away, just let it go. It's amazing how many times three months later they'll say, "Oh, yes, that's great." And I'll say, "Isn't that something you thought about before?" I find that when I pull back, with a little bit of time, it often comes back to the way I envisioned it to begin with. It's just that they need to see most of the room completed before they understand the idea of purple curtains.

MITCHELL OWENS Anyone can have confidence or imagination or background. But possessing one characteristic alone, without at least one of the other two, doesn't really help one, at least not when you are defining the difference between a great designer and a merely good one. Background won't do it alone. Just because you grew up in beautiful houses or are a member of a certain social milieu doesn't mean you can create ravishing rooms. Ditto confidence—confidence without self-control would be disastrous. Ditto imagination—you have to also know how to put that imagination into three-dimensional reality. One could do without the background element, because that can be learned, the nuances and such. Confidence you can learn also, if you've the right mentor to do the pushing. But imagination cannot be acquired; you either possess it or you don't. But in the end, beyond those considerations, what makes a great designer is a great client. If you don't have clients willing to hop on your bandwagon, no successful room can be accomplished, let alone one with genius.

RECOMMENDED READING

Baldwin, Billy. *Billy Baldwin Decorates*. Chartwell Books, 1972.

———. *Billy Baldwin Remembers*. Harcourt Brace and Jovanovich, 1974.

Banks-Pye, Roger, and James Merrell. *International Interiors*. Ryland, Peters and Small, 2005.

Becker, Robert. *Nancy Lancaster, Her Life, Her World, Her Art*. Knopf, 1996.

Bilhuber, Jeffrey, and Annette Tapert. *Design Basics: Expert Solutions for Designing the House of Your Dreams*. Rizzoli, 2003.

Bowden-Smith, Rosemary. *The Chinese Pavilion*. Avenue Publishing, 1988.

Bowles, Hamish. *Vogue Living: Houses, Gardens, People*. Knopf, 2007.

Capote, Truman. *Observations*. Simon and Schuster, 1995.

Chananx, Adolphe. *Jean Michel Frank*. Editions du Regard, 1980.

Cliff, Stafford. *The Way We Live*. Clarkson Potter, 2003.

Connolly, Cyril and Jerome Zerbe. *Le Pavilons. French Pavilions of the Eighteenth Century*. Hamish Hamilton, 1962.

Cornforth, John. *English Interiors 1790-1848: The Quest for Comfort*. Barrie & Jenkins, 1978.

Crater, Susan Bartlett, and Apple Parish Bartlett. *Sister: The Life of Legendary American Interior Decorator Mrs. Henry Parish II*. St. Martin's Press, 2000.

Draper, Dorothy. *Decorating Is Fun*. Doubleday, 1939.

Ede, Jim. *A Way of Life, Kettle's Yard*. Cambridge University Press, 1984.

Editors of House and Garden. *House and Garden's Best in Decoration*. Random House, 1987.

Frengnac, Claude. *The Great Houses of Paris*. Littlehampton Book Services, 1979.

Guest, C. Z. *First Garden*. G. P. Putnam, 1970.

Hadley, Albert. *Drawings and the Design Process*. New York School of Interior Design, 2004.

Hampton, Mark. *Mark Hampton on Decorating*. Random House, 1989.

Hicks, David. *Living with Design*. Morrow, 1979.

Johnson, Jay. *Jed Johnson, Opulent Restraint*. Rizzoli, 2005.

Jones, Chester. *Colefax and Fowler: The Best in Interior Design*. Barrie & Jenkins, 1989.

Lees-Milne, Avilde. *The Englishman's Room*. Salem House Publications, 1989.

Leveque, Jean, editor. *Jansen Decoration*. Soc/Etudes/Publishing Economiques, 1971.

Lewis, Adam. *Albert Hadley, the Story of America's Preeminent Interior Designer*. Rizzoli, 2005.

Mongiardino, Renzo. *Roomscapes*. Rizzoli International Publications, 2001.

Montgomery-Massingburd, Hugh. *Great Houses of England and Wales*. Rizzoli International Publications, 1994.

Parish, Sister, Albert Hadley, and Christopher Petankas. *Parish-Hadley: Sixty Years of American Design*. Little, Brown & Company, 1995.

Phillips, Ian, and Angelika Taschen. *New Seaside Interiors*. Taschen, 2008.

Plumb, Barbara. *Horst Interiors*. Little, Brown & Company, 1993.

Pratt, Richard. *David Adler, the Architect and His Work*. M. Evans & Company, 1970.

Praz, Mario. *The House of Life*. Methuen, 1964.

Salney, Stephen M. *Michael Taylor: Interior Design*. W.W. Norton and Company, 2009.

Schina, Marina. *Visions of Paradise*. Stewart, Tabori & Chang, 1985.

Silver, Nathan. *Lost in New York*. Mariner Books, 2000.

Smith, Jane S. *Elsie de Wolfe*. Atheneum, 1982.

Stephanidis, John. *John Stephanidis Living by Design*. Rizzoli, 1997.

Surka, Norma. *The New York Times Book of Interiors and Decorations*. HarperCollins, 1978.

Taschen, Angelika. *Provence Style*. Taschen, 2008.

Taylor, Patrick, and Jacques Wirtz. *Wirtz Gardens. 2004 Exhibitions*. International/Wirtz International, 2004.

Thorne, Martha, editor, and Richard Guy Wilson, Pauline Metcalf, Ghenete Zelleke. *David Adler, Architect: The Elements of Style*. Yale University Press, 2002.

Tweed, Katherine. *The Finest Rooms by America's Great Decorators*. Viking, 1964.

Vervoordt, Axel. *Timeless Interiors*. Flammarion, 2007.

Webber, Bruce. *A House Is Not a Home*. Bulfinch Press, 1996.

Wharton, Edith, Ogden Codman, Jr., and Richard Guy Wilson. *The Decoration of Houses*. Rizzoli, 2007.

Whiton, Sherrill. *Interior Design and Decoration*. Lippincott, 1974.

Williams, Bunny. *An Affair with a House*. Stewart, Tabori and Chang, 2005.

Wood, Martin. *John Fowler: Prince of Decorators*. Frances Lincoln, 2007.

―――. *Nancy Lancaster: English Country House Style*. Frances Lincoln, 2005.

CONTRIBUTORS

MARTHA ANGUS incorporates a modern sensibility with a classical design approach that is well informed and timeless. She studied at the École des Beaux-Arts in France, Carnegie Mellon University, and Sotheby's Restoration in New York.

JEFFREY BILHUBER has a uniquely American perspective that breathes new life into traditionalism with a confirmed understanding of modern sensibilities. He is the author of *Defining Luxury: The Qualities of Life at Home* (Rizzoli).

MARIO BUATTA was dubbed "The Prince of Chintz" and has been a household name in design for years. He has a client list that has included names like Henry Ford II and Charlotte Ford.

EMMA BURNS began her decorating career with Colefax & Fowler. Prior to that she worked for the London-based interior decorating firm Charles Hammond. Ms. Burns lives in both London and Oxfordshire.

JANE CHURCHILL is internationally famous for her elegant interiors. Combining classical and contemporary elements, she works closely with her clients and has a vast portfolio of projects all over the world.

PETER DUNHAM set up his own interior design firm after fifteen years in real estate. He designs a collection of furnishing fabrics that are sold in twenty showrooms, and more recently he opened his own shop, Hollywood at Home.

CAROLYN ENGLEFIELD has had an impressive career as an editor. She was with *House & Garden* magazine for two years and spent fourteen years with *House Beautiful,* where she was senior editor. She joined *Veranda* magazine in 2000 and became editor-at-large in 2007.

ALBERT HADLEY is known as the dean of American interior design. He was first a student and then a professor at the Parsons School of Design. He worked with Eleanor Brown at McMillen Inc. before beginning his partnership with Sister Parish at the influential firm Parish-Hadley Associates.

WILLIAM HODGINS was educated at the Parsons School of Design. After five years with Parish-Hadley Associates he relocated to Boston, where he established his own firm in 1968. Since then, he has chosen to concentrate exclusively on residential projects for clients including, among others, the Taubmans and the Goulds.

KATHRYN IRELAND blends English manor and French farmhouse sensibilities with Santa Monica's bohemian vibe. She created signature interiors for a distinguished clientele, ranging from David Mamet to Caroline Kennedy Schlossberg. Her fabric collection is distributed in top U.S. showrooms as well as in her namesake London showroom.

CATHY KINCAID's traditional style evokes a sense of comfortable elegance that remains unmatched. She offers a diverse combination of old and new design elements, but her primary goal as a designer remains to create inviting, livable spaces with her clients' happiness the top priority.

BRIAN McCARTHY began his decorating career at Parish-Hadley in 1983 as Albert Hadley's assistant. He then established Brian J. McCarthy, Inc., in 1992 and has gone on to decorate homes all over the United States. He operates an office in Paris to support his love of European furniture and decorative arts.

JOSIE McCARTHY is a Dallas-based interior decorator. She's designed interiors for more than thirty years with clients across the United States. She creates timeless interiors that combine comfort with elegance, ranging from traditional to modern.

MITCHELL OWENS is the executive editor of *Elle Decor* and a former design and style columnist for *The New York Times*. He has edited several design books, including *Elsie de Wolfe: The Birth of Modern Interior Decoration* (Acanthus, 2005) and *Jansen* (Acanthus, 2006).

MILES REDD attended the Parsons School of Design and New York University, studying fashion and film. He founded his interior decorating firm in 1998 after working for both John Rosselli and Bunny Williams. In 2003 he was named creative director of Oscar de la Renta Home.

SUZANNE RHEINSTEIN is an interior designer based in Los Angeles. She is the owner of Hollyhock, a shop full of quirky one-of-a-kind pieces, antiques, and her bespoke line of upholstery, occasional furniture, and lighting. She is best known for designing houses for today's families, with handsome antique furniture and a traditional sense of comfort.

TODD ROMANO began his career seventeen years ago as an assistant for Mario Buatta. He founded his design firm and eponymous shop on Lexington Avenue in 1999. He has been named to numerous lists of the Top 100 Best Decorators in America and recently opened an expanded showroom version of his shop in the Fine Arts Building in New York.

DANIEL ROMUALDEZ is an architect based in New York, whose office also provides interior decoration services. He was born in the Philippines and spent his undergraduate years at Yale. While at Yale, he was exposed to both the work and clients of Sister Parish. He has been a fan of hers ever since.

JOHN ROSSELLI opened his first shop in New York City fifty years ago, and it immediately became a destination for those in the world of design and decoration. His name has since come to represent affordable antiques with a decorative, even whimsical sense of style.

TOM SCHEERER has practiced architecture and interior design in Manhattan since 1985. His work is characterized by clear and logical architectural solutions combined with beautiful, comfortable furnishings. He emphasizes furniture planning, spatial relationships, color, and texture over the ornate or purely decorative.

SUZANNE TUCKER holds a BFA in design from UCLA. She worked in London for several years before returning to California, where she became the protégée of the legendary Michael Taylor, whose business she now owns with her partner Timothy Marks. *Architectural Digest* has honored Suzanne as one of the AD 100 Top Designers in the World.

CARLETON VARNEY is CEO of Dorothy Draper & Company, Inc., one of the oldest established decorating firms in America, founded by the legendary Dorothy Draper. Mr. Varney was the design consultant to the White House during the Carter administration and is the author of twenty-six books, including *Houses in My Heart*.

DAVID WEBSTER is president of Webster and Company, a multiline to the trade showroom at the Boston Design Center. His design philosophy is: "First of all, be CREATIVE; secondly, don't be afraid to break some rules; lastly, have fun in the process!"

BUNNY WILLIAMS opened her own interior design company in 1988 after twenty-two years with Parish-Hadley Associates. She co-owns Treillage, a garden furniture and ornament shop in New York, with her husband, antiques dealer John Rosselli. She is author of *An Affair with a House*.

PAUL VINCENT WISEMAN and his firm the Wiseman Group have been in the interior design business for almost thirty years. Paul is always included in the Architectural Digest 100 Best Designers list and has been the ASID (American Society of Interior Designers) Designer of the Year.

ACKNOWLEDGMENTS

We started this project as a classic book on decorating illustrated with photographs of houses we loved. We brought it to our friend Charlie Spicer at St. Martin's Press, who got the ball rolling for us with our editor BJ Berti. With the support of the esteemed head of St. Martin's Press, Sally Richardson, BJ transformed the project into a book on decorating illustrated with watercolors. Her creative input and wonderful advice every step of the way helped shape the book into its final form, and we are most grateful for her support and encouragement. BJ and executive art director Michael Storrings are responsible for the beautiful cover, and Gretchen Achilles, with Michelle McMillian and James Sinclair, are responsible for the lovely design of the book interior.

As we began to gather our thoughts on decorating, it struck us that our thoughts were repetitive and we were creating another "how to" guide that would be skimmed through and put aside after a quick read. The idea came to us to include multiple voices on design and to create a conversation, where many points of view would be represented. We wanted not only to discuss a variety of approaches, but also to reveal what the process is like working with a top decorator. This led us to interview the venerable list of designers, editors, and showroom owners from across the United States and Britain who contributed to this book. We are incredibly grateful for their time and participation. The thread that ties the group together is obviously the quality of their work, but it is also, and maybe more important, their absolute love of design. What emerged every time we started the interviews was their total delight in what they do. Their childhood stories all started to sound the same: "I was pushing the living room furniture around when I was ten and bought my first painting from a junk shop when I was eleven. I started collecting when I was twelve and insisted my mother paint my room orange or blue or yellow," and so on. As a group, they are conversant in all aspects of design, have studied all of the greats who came before them, know periods of furniture like the back of their hand, and are fueled by curiosity and exposure. We cannot thank them enough for their generosity and willingness to share the tools of their trade.

Finally, the book's ultimate transformation took place when we met the amazing watercolorist and now good friend Mita Corsini Bland. It was serendipity that brought us to Mita, and it is her beautiful paintings that bring our ideas on decorating to life. We are eternally grateful for her art, her friendship, and her contributions on every level to the book.

Our gratitude goes to other friends who helped read, comment, and offer other forms of support: Albert Hadley, David Michaelis, Jennifer Maguire Isham, Sarah Wadsworth, Clara Bingham, Susie Lodge, Karen Wolter, John Derian, William Ivey Long, Mitchell Owens, Mario Buatta, and Gerald Bland. And to our families, who could always be counted on for opinions and support, and, of course, to Sister, who provided the inspiration that is responsible for our continuing love of houses and all that goes into them.